# THE
# EXTRAORDINARY POWER
## OF
# KINDNESS

## TRUE STORIES THAT WILL ENRICH, ENCOURAGE, AND INSPIRE YOU.

*GOD BLESS you*
*Bill*

## BILL SCHIEBLER

# THE EXTRAORDINARY POWER OF
# KINDNESS

Copyright © 2017 Bill Schiebler
www.billschiebler.com

All rights reserved. This book is protected by the copyright laws of the United States of America. No part of this book may be reproduced, stored in a retrievable manner, or transmitted in any form without the written permission of the author, except in the case of brief quotations embodied in critical articles and reviews. For permissions, contact info@billschiebler.com.

Unless otherwise indicated, all Scripture quotations are taken from the New King James Version®. Copyright © 1982 by Thomas Nelson. Used by permission. All rights reserved.

ISBN 10: 1974097420
ISBN 13: 978-1974097425

For additional copies of this or other books by Bill Schiebler,
go to his website at www.billschiebler.com.

### Editing/Book Design
Editing, cover design, and book design services were provided by Ronald Olson.
He can be reached at ron@ronaldolson.com.

# READERS WRITE ABOUT
## *The Extraordinary Power of KINDNESS*

*This isn't a goody-two-shoes book; it's jam-packed with profound experiences. Our family is rereading it for the third time. Each time, more great lessons of wisdom and kindness jump out at us.*

Colonel Hilton J.
Alexandria, VA

*This book was an absolute page turner. I couldn't put it down. When your 17-year-old will actually listen and then talk about a book you're reading, it speaks volumes.*

Tammy B.
Burnsville, MN

*Throughout my life, I've read very few books non-stop, but this is one of them. It was thrilling! I shed tears as I read this book.*

Larry B.
Webb, IA

*Once you pick up this book to read, you won't want to put it down. Personally, I don't think people could read this book without their life being changed for the better.*

Howard T.
Asheville, NC

*I so wish this book was a mandatory high school read. If so, I think the world would be a better place.*

Signy L.
San Antonio, TX

*The timing of this book is good as it addresses the tremendous need for kindness in our lives and country. The simple and powerful stories will touch and change the heart of each person who reads this book.*

Bob M.
Rhinelander, WI

*As one who has conducted a prison ministry since retiring from military service, this book should be placed into the hands of every convict in prisons. I say kindness would pave the way for less recidivism!*

Brigadier General Tom B. (Retired)
Fort Bragg, NC

*As you read through these stories, you begin to see yourself. I wept. I laughed. But in the end, I was never more encouraged to meet the Holy Spirit and touch fingers with His amazing kindness.*

Pastor Tom F.
Eden Prairie, MN

# ACKNOWLEDGEMENTS

Over the years, I feel exceedingly fortunate to have met and known some terrific people. I'd like to thank a few of them who have given me great inspiration by helping me gain enough confidence to write down some of my stories.

Former President Dwight Eisenhower and his wife Mamie sat me down one time and asked me to promise them that I'd always write from my heart. I have tried to always follow their advice. *(Read about this story in the Afterword.)*

There is no way I could have written this book without the help of my editor, Ron Olson. He has watched over me like a watchdog and helped make sense out of everything I wrote.

And now, I saved the best for last. Bonnie Gavin, my wife, has stood by my side, keeping her patience as I have often struggled to find the right words to convey my messages. She has proven to be most incisive, teaching me how to "look at both sides of a coin." Bonnie never wavers with her enthusiasm. She has been my greatest encourager.

# TABLE OF CONTENTS

# FOREWORD

As Bill began writing this book, General John W. Vessey, Jr., the former chairman of the Joint Chiefs of Staff, offered to write the foreword. Sadly, he passed away before the book was finished, so I am especially honored and privileged to have this opportunity to introduce you to my hero, Bill Schiebler, and his wonderful book.

In my 13-year NFL football career with the Minnesota Vikings, I had the opportunity to play in the Super Bowl and to meet and play against some of the greatest players in the world, many of whom are now in the Hall of Fame. I also met Muhammad Ali, who had the nickname "The Greatest," and was ranked as the greatest athlete of the 20th Century by Sports Illustrated magazine. Later, I had the opportunity to have dinner with him and acted as his personal bodyguard when he fought against Lyle Alzado in an exhibition bout in 1979.

With all that said, in my 64 years of life, I have never met a more humble, kind, and giving person than Bill. In my world, *he* is the greatest. He exemplifies courage every day of his life as he battles against multiple sclerosis, which seems to lay a new challenge before him each day. He inspires and encourages me to never quit and to keep fighting the good fight.

Bill served in the United States Army Rangers during the Vietnam War, and was a paratrooper and infantry rifle platoon leader. He was among the greatest fighting men of their day. If one could imagine Bill during the time of King David in the Old Testament, he would be known as one of "God's mighty men of valor!"

I'm humbled to be chosen as the one to introduce you to this man and this amazing book. In it, Bill shares several stories from his life that show how the power of kindness transforms and enriches our lives. I have personally experienced his incredible kindness over the years. He has always had my back no matter what, and has been there for me and my entire family.

Words could never describe my love for this mighty man of valor and kindness! Truly, his strength and kindness has transformed and enriched the lives of many people. Even though he has been off the field of battle for many years, he continues to fight the good fight for the Greatest Hero we all need, Jesus Christ!

Spend some time in this book! Read it through and soak up what's written in its pages. Immerse yourself in the stories. It's truly amazing to read about the fascinating, intriguing, and challenging life this man has led. He has not only survived, but thrived! I sat there awestruck and in tears as I read these eight riveting stories, which give you just a few glimpses into his remarkable life.

As you read each story, you will begin to see how important it is to show kindness to others. It is a redeeming quality that can be expressed in a variety of ways. You will be challenged and encouraged to muster up your own creative ideas in this area with the help of the Holy Spirit.

Wait until you read how Bill follows his grandfather's advice and ends up saving hundreds of lives as a result. Then, hang on as you read the story of Tony and dare to put yourself in his place. And take note of the creative way Bill tackled, head-on, his encounter with bullying, a pervasive problem that today runs rampant throughout our schools, our society, and over the Internet.

This book is a life changing read for all ages. I think it is especially good for parents to read and pass on to their children and their children's children, as it teaches lessons on the power of kindness that can influence generations to come. I know that everyone who reads this book will be impacted, blessed, and transformed by entering into these stories from the life of my friend and hero, Bill Schiebler.

*Mark Mullaney, Sr.*

# INTRODUCTION

Life sometimes takes us on unexpected, crazy turns. There's no way to fully prepare for what happens to us. As I look back, I chuckle at the unforeseen routes I've taken with my own life. This book is a perfect example of that.

After receiving two college degrees and doing graduate work, thuh wurst grayds eye've evir receeved wur inn englisch, grammurr, compohsitiun, writng, and speling.

If anybody would have ever told me I'd wind up writing this book (or any book for that matter), I'd just shake my head and reply, "You're crazy."

For some people, simply trying to write a few fascinating stories would be enough, but that was not my intention when I sat down to write this book. The stories I've included portray some of the most profound experiences I've had throughout my life. And each one taught me a lesson in kindness.

When I was younger, I didn't give much thought to the attribute of kindness. It was simply an attitude that was instilled in me while growing up. But over the years, I have had so many different experiences that have allowed me to see the result of kindness that I felt compelled to write down some of my stories.

You have no idea how profoundly you can affect another by lending them a helping hand. Regardless of whether your gesture is reciprocated, when you show kindness to another, you will enrich yourself.

In my view, though, I think kindness is something that needs to be learned. If you are a kind person, most likely you learned this trait from the example of others.

If you were with me today, you'd probably ask me, "Well, Bill, then who taught you to be kind to others?"

It doesn't take long for me to answer that question. My mother and dad taught me.

My dad was the oldest of six children, born way back in 1901 in Wisconsin. As German immigrants, during World War I my dad's family was viewed with distrust and treated with incredible meanness. But in the midst of that, his father repeatedly reminded them to turn the other cheek and to remember that they were fortunate to be living in the greatest country in the world.

His father taught my dad and the other children to reach out to those unfriendly people and to be kind to them. As a result, their family was finally accepted and became good friends with their neighbors.

Thanks to the lessons he learned growing up, my dad was one of the kindest people I have ever known. He was a wonderful example to us children and taught us this priceless attribute through his words and kind, gentlemanly ways.

My mother was also the oldest of six children, born in 1904 in

Lowell, Massachusetts. Lowell was a cotton and wool milling town along the Merrimac River. Folks called that area the "mile of mills," and many of the families were dirt poor.

In the winter, folks were forced to keep temperatures barely above freezing at home because they couldn't afford to buy very much coal. Conditions were so dismal that some of the children who worked in the mills had to sleep beside the huge milling machines at night because the steam and rollers gave off enough heat to keep those factories (and them) somewhat warm. At times, children even had to scrape grease off the rollers to put on their bread because the families couldn't afford butter. Those horrendous conditions became the scene for the first child labor laws in the United States.

Times got rough for my mother's family, as well. When she was only 14 years old, her own mother died and her dad had no option but to sit her down for a serious talk.

"Mary," he began. "You're not going to be able to finish high school. You will have to do all of the housecleaning, cooking and sewing for your five younger brothers and sisters. Our family can't possibly afford to stay together unless you will help all of us."

Somehow, with sheer grit and endless creativity, my mother managed to get three of her five siblings through college. Then, when she was 32, my mother went back to graduate from high school. She put herself through college and went on to teach gifted children in the Boston School District.

When I was a youngster, mother would take me along on some of her forays to the homes of impoverished people who, surprisingly, lived less than a mile away from our house. She delighted in taking shopping bags filled with groceries over to those needy folks. And I experienced how thrilled those recipients of kindness became when we brightened their day.

My mother passed on a useful phrase that I have used throughout my life. Whenever I am confronted by someone who needs help, I stop and ask myself her simple, four word question: "What would Jesus do?"

Has every act of kindness turned out the way I wanted? Of course not. Sometimes my kind acts were rejected, and other times they even blew up in my face. But may I make one suggestion to you? Open your heart as you read these stories and always expect the best! The experiences I've had demonstrate how showing kindness to another can have a powerful, positive, life-changing effect, not just on them, but especially on you.

*Bill Schiebler*

*You cannot do
a kindness too soon,
for you never know how
soon it will be too late.*

Ralph Waldo Emerson
Essayist, Poet

# 1

# TONY

*The kindness of a seasoned combat nurse brings an eternal reward.*

During World War II, the Germans successfully developed one of the deadliest and most accurate artillery pieces known to man. The 88mm flak gun had such incredible velocity that the trajectory of its shell was practically flat, unlike the arc of most artillery shells.

At first, the 88 shells had so much velocity that they literally went all the way through tanks before exploding on their backside. Sadistic German SS commanders came up with a sinister idea; they merely toned down the 88's velocity so its shells would explode inside the tanks.

When a German 88 shell hit an Allied tank, there was nothing left but smoldering ruins. It was an exercise in futility to try to identify anybody inside a tank that had been hit by an 88's deadly shells. There were no remains, only mincemeat! The

88s were so deadly accurate because the Germans originally designed the guns for anti-aircraft duty in places where it was needed.

It is not my intention to go into all the gory details about such a deadly war machine. Instead, I want you to realize the power of this weapon and how it so deeply affected the critically wounded man whose story I am about to tell.

When I was hospitalized at the old Minneapolis Veterans Hospital back in 1985, one morning I unknowingly got off the elevator on the wrong floor. I didn't realize that I was on the second floor instead of the fourth floor where my room was.

As I walked into what I thought was my room, I smelled the horrible stench of defecation. It even permeated the hallway. As I entered this room I saw a horrifying sight! Here was a stump of a man lying there who had just defecated in his diaper, making a mess of the bed. Nurses were cleaning him up.

He had no arms, no legs and was blind!

The sight was too much for me to witness! I immediately turned around and left the room, walking briskly back to the elevator.

My eyes filled with tears as I made my way to the elevator. When its door opened, fortunately there was only a young nurse in it. As she closed the door and pressed the button for the proper floor, she noticed me crying and asked, "What's wrong?"

"Nothing," I mumbled, foolishly thinking that big guys don't cry. Then I really started sobbing!

All at once, she pressed the STOP button. Those were the days of the old-style elevators and we found ourselves stopped between floors.

"Something is dreadfully wrong," she exclaimed. "Now, tell me about it!"

When I told her about the ghastly sight I had just seen, she, too, broke down and began to weep. This young nurse went on to tell me that she had been working in the Veterans Hospital for over four years but hadn't seen anything like what I had just described.

What neither of us knew was that this man was going to be in this hospital for only a few days before being transferred to a more specialized hospital where they treat some of the country's most battered veterans.

As I finally reached my room, I sat on the edge of the bed and thought, *Schiebs, you dummy, you get right back down there to say hello and visit that man! He surely needs to have somebody talk to him.*

Was I going to be in for a surprise! Mustering some courage, I went back down the two floors to see him and found myself talking to a remarkable gentleman whose name was Tony. This man had been lying in hospital beds in this condition for over 40 years!

Since he obviously had no way to help himself, attendants had to clean him up after he went to the bathroom. Others had to tune in his radio, hand feed him and turn on a nearby television set in the room so he could at least listen to it. Having no arms or legs was bad enough. Being totally blind made him utterly dependent on others.

We had quite a visit that first day. Tony was amazingly candid with me from the very start. He asked me, "I'll bet you were a bit taken aback when you first saw me, weren't you?"

Looking down at the floor, I sheepishly admitted that I had stumbled to the elevator door, gotten in and then broke down crying.

Tony was so reassuring to me. Here I was, the one who was supposed to be cheering him up, but he was lifting my spirits.

Finally, I got up the gumption to ask what had happened to him. He told me that back in 1943 in North Africa, he had been fighting the Germans in the desert. His American buddies had just nonchalantly walked through a pass with absolutely no German resistance.

Suddenly, unexpectedly, the silence was shattered! A nearby camouflaged German Tiger Tank and a German 88 anti-tank gun both opened fire. An 88 shell pierced the Allied tank he was walking behind before exploding, practically point-blank, right in front of him!

Tony was ripped to shreds! It was so bad, other soldiers didn't think he had survived and he was left for dead on the battlefield. Fortunately, a seasoned medic noticed some twitching in his stomach and attempted to stabilize him.

Tony was carefully laid on a stretcher. He was bleeding to death and they reached a nearby medic aid station just in time. Thanks to superb battlefield medical care, doctors, nurses and medics saved him.

His medical recovery and route back to the United States consisted of a long progression of stops through several other field hospitals in North Africa.

He had barely stabilized when he was finally evacuated by a medical ship that steamed quietly, and without any lights on, out through the Straits of Gibraltar. This was a dangerous trip, as German U-boats laid in wait at periscope depth, poised to torpedo unsuspecting Allied ships attempting to pass through the perilous Straits.

He finally reached England where doctors were barely able to keep him alive. Months passed before he was stabilized enough to be put on a larger hospital troop ship that sailed back to the United States to safe harbor in New York City.

From there, he was transferred to the large Naval Battery Hospital in Boston where he lingered for months, still clinging to life. This hospital specialized in helping critical care soldiers adjust to the reality of what, for them, would be basic survival.

It was to be more than two years later, after World War II had ended, when he was finally put on a troop train and transported to a much smaller Veterans Administration hospital in North Dakota, his home state.

*(Why have I elaborated so thoroughly on Tony's slow evacuation route? In those days a soldier's gradual trip home, whether he had been wounded or not, had a much more stabilizing effect on him than the rapid, present-day evacuation practice. Now, a soldier can be fighting one day in a far-away country, and a few days later find himself back home walking into a neighborhood drug store where the*

*pharmacist, customers and check-out clerks are oblivious to a war being fought in another part of the world.*

*Such rapid readjustment is far too strenuous for many of us combat veterans. I believe this is one of the major reasons for the alarming, progressive rate of Post-Traumatic Stress Disorder.)*

Tony had been raised on a farm, but most of his family had spread out across the country prior to the war. Although certain family members were reached, they couldn't do anything about visiting him, as the hospital was way too far away from them.

Traveling long distances without much public transportation was a problem during World War II. At best, any journey became difficult and strenuous for anyone. Many families had barely survived the Great Depression, and they lived practically out of touch from civilization, isolated in small pockets throughout the Plains States. Their plight had been greatly exacerbated by the onset of the war, and Tony's family was no exception.

Unfortunately, what little hope or optimism he had was immediately dashed to the ground barely two weeks after arriving in North Dakota.

Tony's wife appeared one morning, unannounced, to visit him. She took one brief look at him and was horrified. Upon seeing such a ghastly sight, she shrieked and hurried out of the room, crying. She abruptly ran down the hospital corridor, screaming, "I can't take this! I can't take this!"

That was the last time Tony ever heard her voice. She never saw Tony again.

Not much time went by before divorce papers arrived one morning. Tony couldn't see his nurse, but she had tears in her eyes as she regretfully read the summons to him.

Now even that hope was gone. His wife's rejection sent him into deep depression. Tony's bouts of quiet trembling became so severe that he just lay there shaking, without uttering a word. Others attended to him, but it seemed as if they were attending to a practically lifeless body.

For months, Tony went through sullen bouts of absolute silence. The silence was only broken when he shouted sarcastic epithets at anybody who attempted to help him.

One day, his dismal disposition was changed.

He was confronted by an elderly combat nurse who had spent time on remote islands in the Pacific helping others who had been as severely wounded (both physically and mentally) as Tony.

She snapped at him, "Get hold of yourself! I'm sick of your attitude!"

She rolled Tony over, face down, pushing his head next to his own excrement. Tony was now in the most serious bind he had been in since being hit. He started to gag but there was no way out of it for him. He felt he was literally smothering in his own feces.

Fortunately, there was a compassionate side to "the old battle axe" (as he later called her). She let Tony wallow in his own misery for only a few moments, just long enough to knock some sense into his blockheaded skull.

Then she changed her demeanor as if a coin had been flipped from one side to the other.

She turned Tony over on his back so he could breathe and then lovingly wiped off his face. As she elevated his head on a clean pillow, she kissed him gently on his forehead and sat down to softly reassure him.

Her name was Clarice. "Would you like to have me read to you?" she asked.

Tony was so shook up that he couldn't muster words to reply. The ex-soldier who was trapped in the jumbled remains of a human body had met his match. This elderly nurse was determined to help him.

She lovingly laughed, then exclaimed, "I've got an idea. Is it all right if I read a story to you from my Bible? It's from a book called Luke. This is a moving story about gratitude. I'll turn to the seventeenth chapter where it talks about ten men who are healed of leprosy. Unfortunately, only one man comes back to say thanks. This story really shows us the importance of being grateful."

As she finished reading the Bible story to Tony, she spoke to him from her heart.

"Tony, you've got to be grateful that you're still alive. Somehow, I get a strong feeling that since you've survived this horrific encounter with death, you're going to find a way to make do with what you have left–your life AND your sanity. First of all, though, you've got to work on building up your spirituality, your faith in God. He is the One who can give meaning to your life.

"I so hope you enjoyed the story I read to you. Better yet, I'll come by to see you each night after I get off work and if you'd like, I'll read other fascinating stories to you from my Bible."

One night in the middle of December, the nurse said to Tony, "Here's what I'll do, I'll read to you a story about Christmas. I don't know if you have any spiritual beliefs, but this will explain why Christians celebrate Christmas at this time of the year."

Though Christmas passed, each night she continued to lovingly read Bible stories to Tony until he had fallen asleep. For months, Tony would merely lie there motionless. He didn't even acknowledge or thank her.

But she was getting through to him — and she knew it!

This elderly nurse wouldn't give up on him. It was as if she was bound and determined to get through to Tony. Each time she was on duty, she would enter his room, cheerfully greeting him and sometimes even bringing in another nurse to say hello.

Since Tony had no hand to hold, each woman would gently place her hands upon his shoulders to give him hugs of reassurance and a gentle kiss. Not known to Tony was that his nurse was the very same nurse who had been forced to read his divorce papers to him.

Clarice was a loving woman, compassionate enough to realize that Tony needed at least one friend in his restricted, gloomy world. Her touch, that little bit of human compassion, was what saved Tony.

It took months for him to come out of his severe depression, but she kept it up, gently putting her hands on his shoulder while quietly reading and reassuring him that she was there to be his friend.

After all this time of Clarice's Bible reading and kindness, Tony finally reached a point of curiosity. One morning he asked if she could arrange to have some clergy from different religions come in to visit with him. He wanted them to tell him about their particular religion.

You see, Tony, like the rest of us combat veterans, was beginning to wonder about his very existence. He was wondering why he had been spared. Why hadn't it been him inside that tank where its men were decimated? His mind was spinning wildly with all sorts of unanswered questions.

Clarice jumped at the opportunity and really went to bat for Tony. She saw to it that Christians, a Buddhist monk, a Muslim, a Jewish Rabbi, a Protestant minister, a Catholic priest and nun, a Mormon (the list went on and on) and even a well-known atheist in the area came in to see Tony. Each of them explained their spiritual and philosophical views and answered his numerous questions.

If you were merely observing this seemingly never-ending line of visitors, you could wrongfully conclude that the whole arena of religion and spirituality was quite confusing to Tony. That was not the case. He had a sharp, logical mind and sorted out all those differing views.

After weeks of pondering what all those people had shared with him, one morning Tony asked for his special nurse-friend to come to see him. He wanted to tell her he had made up his mind about religion and spirituality. His search had finally come to an end.

Though off-duty that day, Clarice sped in to the hospital to see him as soon as she could. As she pulled up a chair for the momentous occasion, his answer was surprisingly, compellingly, very simple. He had decided to become a Christian!

"Why?" she asked.

He answered her in a forthright manner. "Because Christianity was the only religion that praised and worshipped somebody who was *alive*. All of those others were worshiping someone who was *dead*. Nobody had come back to life except Jesus Christ. He not only died for our sins, He came back to life and never died again. And when He ascended into Heaven, there were 300 to 500 people who watched Him go."

Tony was brilliant! He superbly displayed a very clear view of faith. In his research by visiting with others, he simply concluded that because so many other people saw Jesus as He had gone up into Heaven that Jesus was the only person Tony knew of who had risen from the dead.

She just shook her head in amazement at Tony's reasoning. He had made up his mind, and that was that.

Gradually, after all those months of soul-searching, Tony had emerged as a different man. Somehow, he developed an incredible sense of humor! Here was a man who could even laugh at himself in spite of his wretched condition. One time, he even asked one of the nurses out on a *blind date!* Everybody, especially Tony, had a good laugh about his request!

As for me, although my contact with Tony only lasted for a few days, we jam-packed a lot of deep discussions into that time. I began to feel as though I had known Tony for a very long time. He was such an uplifting, intriguing person that I found myself spending any spare moments I had visiting with him.

One morning we talked about those miserable early days before he had decided on his own to become a follower of Jesus Christ. I knew that God promises to make all situations, no matter how bad they appear, work for good, but I didn't know what Tony believed. I asked him whether he had ever considered suicide. His answer was humorous, simple, and classic Tony.

"Yup," he said. "At first, I sure did contemplate suicide, but quickly realized I was locked into this wretched body. I couldn't hold a pistol against my head because I had no hand to do so. I couldn't walk into a garage to hang myself because I had no legs to do so. I sighed in resignation. I finally realized I would be lying here for a long, long time. So, the first thing I promised myself was that I wouldn't lose my sanity.

"Wouldn't you know it? It was that very morning, barely 15 minutes later, when my nurse, Clarice, walked into my room. She chewed me out and rolled me over to give me a taste of my own medicine. That morning, though, she saved my life, not only physically, but spiritually.

"I came to realize that God had a purpose for me and I had no right to even think about suicide."

Early one afternoon a few days later, just as the shifts were changing, a floor nurse called up to my ward and asked if that man named Bill, the one with those funny jokes and quips, could immediately come down to see his friend, Tony. I grabbed a few jokes and quips I had collected and scampered downstairs to see him.

When I entered his room, there were a couple of doctors, three nurses and some orderlies lined up alongside Tony. I joined the crew. Someone had brought in a festive cake for the occasion. I thought it must be his birthday party, but it wasn't.

We had so much fun laughing and carrying on with Tony, but also taking turns telling him how proud we were of him. I knew he would soon be leaving, but I didn't know it was going to be before I could come back to say a final goodbye.

Early the next morning, I made a special effort to get down and visit with Tony before he left. To my dismay, when I walked into his room to visit him that one last time, Tony was already gone.

Talk about frustration! I just stood there and stared at an empty, newly made-up hospital bed. I was heartbroken, not even getting a chance to say goodbye to my friend. A passing nurse told me he had been transferred to a huge hospital called *Wall* in Milwaukee.

Nine years went by and I nearly lost all hope of ever seeing Tony again.

Some evenings, often late into the night, I visited with various long distance operators trying to find clues about Tony's whereabouts. Sadly, though, since I didn't know his last name, none of them were able to help me. I even attempted to reach him through various veterans' hospitals, but to no avail.

What happened next had to be the Holy Spirit talking to me in a way I couldn't even perceive.

Late one night, just by chance, I was visiting with a very understanding operator whose husband worked at a veteran's hospital. She said, "All of these years, you've been spelling *Wall* wrong! It's not spelled W-A-L-L. It's spelled W-A-H-L. It's a huge hospital in the Milwaukee area where they care for severely handicapped combat veterans. They have recently renamed it Zablocki Hospital in honor of the late congressman, Clement Zablocki, so there is no more Wahl Hospital. Here, let me give you the Zablocki Veterans Hospital's telephone number."

BANG! Was I ever in business now! I couldn't wait to call this hospital's chaplain the first thing in the morning. When I reached him, I gave him Tony's name and description. I told him to look for a rather thin, blind man with curly gray hair, but with no arms and no legs.

Within a few minutes, my phone rang. The chaplain had located my friend, Tony! I was so excited that I jumped in my car and drove all of the way, 300 miles, to Milwaukee.

Nobody knew I was making my journey. I needed to be alone, to be at peace with God. I spent much of my drive thanking the Holy Spirit for giving me the opportunity to reunite at last with my long-lost friend!

When I arrived, I eagerly went upstairs to Tony's ward. Reaching the front desk, Tony's nurses were so friendly to me. One of them exclaimed, "Are you the "Bill" who Tony has often spoken of all these years? We didn't know of a "Bill" in his life. In fact, we never knew of anybody in his life. In these nine long years, to our knowledge, Tony has never had even one visitor."

As I was walking down the aisle to at last see my friend, I joked with one of the nurses who were showing me to his room.

Suddenly, I heard somebody start to scream in one of the rooms. It was Tony! Other nurses dropped what they were doing and rushed in to see what was happening with him.

Tony was shouting with glee! Even after so many years, he still recognized my voice! None of his medical staff had ever seen him respond like that.

Tears came to my eyes. I rushed over to his bunk, lifted him off the bed and sobbed as I hugged him. I wouldn't let him go! Tony started sobbing, too. "Do you know how good it feels to cherish the warmth of a human touch like this?" he exclaimed.

Instantly I replied, "I'm the one who is getting the best end of this deal!"

We visited and carried on. At last, as I was getting ready to leave, he grew strangely quiet. "Well, this is the last time down here I'll see you, Bill. But I'll see you up in Heaven."

Little did I know when I left that this was to be the last time I would see my friend while he was alive. However, I think that somehow he knew.

The hospital medical staff got word to me that he died less than one month later.

As I look back now, I am so thankful that I listened to the prompting of the Holy Spirit and took the time to walk back into Tony's room that morning to talk to him for the first time. Little did I know that those few steps would have such an amazing impact on the rest of my life.

But Tony didn't just touch my life. As the hospital chaplain later told me, "Tony powerfully influenced the lives of almost everyone who encountered this remarkable man."

◆━━━━━━━━━━◆

*Therefore, as the elect of God, holy and beloved,*
*put on tender mercies, kindness, humility, meekness,*
*longsuffering;*
Colossians 3:12

It's not my nature to display what is described in this passage as "tender mercies." After all, I am a seasoned combat veteran, having seen and experienced some of the most horrific situations anyone could imagine. Yet, throughout my life, the very characteristics listed here have shone through my gruff exterior.

This certainly wasn't my own doing. I believe God was using the example of other people in my life to show me how He wants me to act. My mother, my father, and a special grade school teacher were just a few of the many people who impacted my life in positive, godly ways.

Of course, I had some bad examples as well. I remember encountering some people who made me think, *I hope I never treat people the way they do.*

As I look at this list, though, perhaps they do fit me more than

I first thought. For these all describe *strength* of character. It takes a strong person to display these character traits in the midst of difficult circumstances or in the face of an increasingly aggressive society.

But I couldn't do it on my own (and neither could Tony). None of us can. These actually describe the character of Jesus, and it is His Spirit within us that enables them to be seen in a person's life. I certainly couldn't have gone back to Tony's room to talk with him in my own strength. I thank God that He is there to help us whenever we need it.

*Remember,*
*there's no such thing as*
*a small act of kindness.*
*Every act creates a ripple*
*with no logical end.*

Scott Adams
Author, cartoonist

# 2

# FRANCO

*The care of strangers*
*leads a young man into a new life.*

Several years ago, I went out to New Hampshire to see my daughter Linda graduate as an emergency medical technician.

"Dad, while we're out here, why don't we drive up into Maine to see the beautiful scenery and watch the whales?" she asked.

She had a great idea. Maine is beautiful country, but we didn't see much of it on our drive. We had to travel throughout that night into the upper part of the state to reach the scenic coastal town of Bar Harbor in time to catch a whale observation ferry that was leaving at 6:00 a.m. on Sunday.

Linda and I finally arrived around 3:00 a.m., which was too late to check into a motel. She suggested sleeping in the car, so we found a fishing pier and decided to park there. Several cars and trucks were already parked on this large pier that overlooked a number of lobster boats anchored in the harbor.

Linda went to sleep in the back seat, but for some reason I was still wide awake, so I walked over to the edge of the pier and sat down to relax and read my Bible. I perched myself by a huge piling that jutted above the pier.

As I sat there, out of the corner of my eye I noticed a young man who had been sitting by another nearby piling. He seemed quite fidgety. Soon he got up and edged closer to me.

When I finally said hello to him, he returned my greeting in a forlorn manner. To my surprise, he blurted, "Mister, I don't know if I should even talk to you, but I really need advice. It's obvious that you ain't from around here."

He pointed to a fishing boat anchored out about a hundred yards off the pier. "Do you see that boat? Well, that's my lobster trawler. That there fishing boat is all I got. My parents passed away some years ago, and I was the only child in our family. I ain't got nobody! As a kid, I grew up in Lubec, a small fishing village north of here, and lobstering is all I know.

"This is difficult to admit, mister," as he looked down at his feet, "but I'm almost starving to death. The storms out there are so fierce! That last storm almost did me in. Now I'm afraid to go out there again. Mainlanders and you tourist folks have no idea of how scary it is out there."

"What's your name?" I asked.

"Franco."

Pressing for more information, I continued. "How old are you? Have you ever been out of this area?"

"I'm 24," he replied. "The sea is all I've ever known. I've never even been out of Maine. One time, though, I did hitchhike way down to Portland, because my boat's diesel engine went out. They couldn't help me get the parts I needed, but I lucked out and found a re-built engine right here in town. A few of the mechanic guys around here give us fishermen a price break because they know how desperate we are."

At that point, I didn't know what to say. Even though Linda was still sleeping in the car, I'd have to wake her up soon. Somehow I had to help this guy. I wanted to show him some kindness, but giving him just a few bucks wouldn't do.

Suddenly, a creative thought overwhelmed me! It seemed that an idea was forming that might help him, and I realized the Holy Spirit was nudging me.

Motioning toward his anchored trawler I asked, "What have you got out there on your boat?"

He lamented, "Its engine has a built-in transformer to change the current from DC to AC so I can have electricity. I've got an old computer a high school instructor gave me. My most enjoyable hours out at sea are when I'm able to do my computer graphics art work. The printer I own is an old dot-matrix one, but it makes-do. The graphic art pictures I create are about the only items I've got that mean anything to me. They're of no value to anybody else."

"How did you learn so much about computers and graphic art?" I inquired.

For the first time since we had been visiting, he smiled. "I taught myself!" he said proudly.

So I asked him where he lived.

"On my boat," he said matter-of-factly. "It's the only place I've got."

Now I was becoming more curious. "Where do you have your mail sent?" I asked.

He just shrugged his shoulders and stammered, "Who would send me mail?"

"What else do you have on your boat besides your computer and printer?"

"Not much," he admitted, "just a pair of dress blue jeans, my Sunday-best shirt and a newer pair of running shoes. I use 'em for going to church on Sundays. Regardless of what happens, I always come back in to port before Sunday. My dad always said, 'Franco, you've got to respect Almighty God, always!'"

"Are you a Christian?" I inquired.

Confidently, he responded, "Many people around here's Christian."

Drawing closer I asked, "Do you have faith, Franco? I mean real faith?"

Franco smiled again. "Yup. At least I got that!"

This urge to help him was now really compelling me. I challenged him further. "Do you have guts, Franco? I mean real guts?"

His face tightened as he looked to the sea. "Mister, anybody who ventures out there has guts."

My bold idea to help him was now clearly coming to mind. I just might be able to give him some useful advice after all. (I've learned that God often uses one person to help another.) First, though, something was propelling me to really test this fellow.

"Franco, so you've got faith. You say you've got guts. What I'm about to tell you right here is going to take real faith and real guts! Do you have enough courage to improve your lot in life even though you'll have to take drastic measures? Even if it means facing harsher conditions than you've ever known in your life?"

Now I really had his attention. "Mister, just what are you trying to say? You have no idea how dreadful conditions are out there during those storms."

"Try me, Franco," I responded.

"Nobody who hasn't been out on the open sea can possibly know how fierce those storms are. When they hit, I can barely hold on for life! Many times there's nothing I can do but scream, wondering if the next huge wave is going to capsize my boat and drown me!

"Sometimes, I even get reluctant to lift up my lobster traps to see if I've caught anything. When I don't get many of 'em, I just scream again out of frustration. Many times another storm hits before I can sail back to port. It's discouraging.

"I keep being thankful to God, though, for still being alive, grateful for living through my latest nightmare."

He took a deep breath. "Now, though, I've finally reached the point where I'm just tired, too tired of trying to gather enough courage to go back out there again. Even though calms come after the storms, nagging thoughts come over me, and I keep wondering if I'll die when the next one hits. Mister, I never feel free from those disturbing thoughts," he confessed.

The boldness in my voice now even surprised me.

"Franco, you'll need to trust Jesus with what I am about to say. I've never said anything like this to anybody before in my life, but I'm now going to say it to you.

"Get outta here. I mean leave; this morning!"

"But I can't do that," he retorted. "I've got my fishing boat!"

"Who cares?" I snapped back. "Many years ago, I learned a hard but valuable lesson: if something wasn't working, I had to change course. Sometimes I had to resort to drastic measures to make a 180 degree turnaround. This is that time for you, Franco."

Now, he seemed to be groping for a way to make sense of what I was telling him. "What are you saying? What do you want me to do? I can't just leave my fishing boat. It's the only thing I've got!"

"Why can't you leave it?"

It was clear he was beginning to think about it. "Well, what would I do with it?"

"Let me ask you something," I responded. "Is there anything on that boat you'd want to keep?"

Now to my surprise, Franco grinned again. "About the only

thing I can think of is my old computer that I keep wrapped in plastic in the bathroom, although it's not really worth keeping. At least I'd like to take my Bible and my favorite graphic art print-outs. Like I said, when those storms hit, everything gets soaked. I go through rolls of duct tape, covering 'em, making sure those print-outs won't be ruined."

"Is there anything else you'd like to take?" I asked.

"Nothing," he replied quietly as his shoulders seemed to droop under the weight of his circumstances.

Continuing with the advice I was offering Franco was going to require almost as much faith for me to say it as he would need to act on it. I took a deep breath.

"Here goes, Franco. This is going to sound like a crazy, ridiculous idea, but I think you should row back to your fishing boat for one last time, put on your best Sunday jeans and your Sunday shirt, stash an extra pair of skivvies in your pocket, and bid your boat goodbye.

"Say a fervent prayer to Jesus and ask Him to be your best friend. Thank your Heavenly Father for keeping you alive out at sea, and just know that God will watch over you.

"He will, Franco! He will keep you safe. You might not wind up doing what you think you'll do, but He *will* keep you safe."

My own faith was growing as I spoke.

"Leave this life. Walk out of it and then walk into another. Go forward with your new adventure and whatever you do, don't look back. Don't look back, Franco!

"Take a look at your Bible, or as I like to call it, your Survival Manual. In the Old Testament Book of Psalms, the Lord talks about being still. Psalm 46:10 says, 'Be still and know that I am God.' As you read it, think about how the Lord asks us to be still and to trust Him.

"So, Franco, be still. Learn to be calm. Talk with Jesus anytime you start to get anxious. Not only does He want to hear from you, He wants to be your best friend if you will just give Him a chance. But you've got to give Him that chance.

"If you act on what I'm telling you, you will face the greatest challenge you will have ever encountered in your life. But if you trust Jesus, He will watch over you and guide you into a new, thrilling chapter of your life! Jeremiah 29:11 tells us, 'For I know the thoughts that I think toward you,' says the Lord, 'thoughts of peace and not of evil, to give you a future and a hope.'

"If you follow Him, you will find out that the new life He has in store for you will definitely be better than what your miserable life has been up until now. Franco, you can't just think about your plight and wring your hands, wondering what you should do. You've got to take decisive steps to enter a brand new way of living."

Franco was now really listening intently, trying to put all the pieces together in his mind. But I strongly felt I needed to tell him that what I was suggesting was not my idea.

"As you're thinking about what I'm telling you, don't think it is coming from me, Franco. This is coming from the Holy Spirit. I just happen to be His messenger.

"Right now, I'm scratching my head trying to think of anything more I can do to help you, but I have no more time. All I can tell you is what I'd do myself if I was in this predicament. Here is the best advice I can give you.

"Every time you encounter more frustrations and trials, pray to Jesus even more intensely. Ask Him to help you. I don't know what lies ahead for you, Franco, but I do know this: if you don't watch yourself, you'll expend just as much energy being fearful as you will being courageous.

"A lot of people believe an old saying and proclaim that 'they will believe it when they see it.' You're going to have to reverse that saying and put your belief to the test. Franco, you must believe in Jesus first before you will see results. If you do this, He WILL help you! Row back to your boat and gather only your most precious belongings. Then walk off this pier, trek into town and hitchhike out of Bar Harbor and into a brand new world."

"Mister, you really mean that I should leave all of this, don't you?" asked Franco. "What would I do with my fishing boat?"

"As I said before, who cares? Why would anybody want to buy an old, run-down lobster boat these days? I've got to go now or my daughter and I will miss our ferry. It leaves only once a day!"

Linda was now wide awake and wildly waving her arms, motioning me to return to the car. We had to leave to get to the whale observation ferry on time. I gave Franco one of my business cards, said a short prayer with him, asking for God's guidance, and then I hurried back to my car.

That was the last time I ever saw Franco.

One year passed.

Two years passed.

Three years passed.

Then, late one night, my phone rang.

"Mister Schiebler," a man began, as he mispronounced my name. "You probably won't remember me, but my name's Franco. Over three years ago you really helped me."

At this point I vaguely remembered meeting a Franco while out vacationing in Maine, and I remembered some of the conversation we had, but not much else. I did recall how frustrated I felt at the time, not being able to help the kid.

"I do remember you," I replied. "You're the kid I visited with late one night out on a pier in Bar Harbor, Maine. But how did I help you?"

What he was about to tell me would turn out to be one of the most courageous stories I had ever heard.

Franco continued. "After you left me on the pier that early morning, I did what you advised. For one last time, I rowed back to my fishing boat, gathered a few belongings, and then rowed back to the pier where we met. I walked off it, hiked into town and made sure I went to Sunday church for my last time in Bar Harbor."

Franco began telling me an absolutely profound story. "Afterward, I started walking toward the outskirts of town, attempting to hitchhike, but wasn't having any luck.

"Suddenly, one of the town's cop cars pulled over. Out stepped a policeman who recognized me from church. He drove me to a restaurant on the edge of town where truckers congregate, thinking that one of the truckers might give me a lift. I appreciated that kind policeman giving me some help. We said goodbye, then I went into the restaurant.

"What a frustrating experience that was! I just sat there for hours, on into late afternoon, sipping glasses of water.

"It finally came time for the waitresses to change shifts. Before the first one left, though, I could see her clueing in her shift replacement, looking toward me and pointing at the kid who kept asking truckers for a ride.

"Fortunately, I got a more understanding waitress who gave me some stale donuts and a leftover bowl of soup. She winked at me, saying it was 'on the house.' That was the first bit of food I'd had all day.

"She brought them just as I was wondering whether I should just give up on such a foolish idea and head back to my dinghy. But mister, you had said to put my trust in Jesus and not to look back, so I just continued to sit there, wondering what to do. It was getting to be late afternoon and the sun was going down.

"To my surprise, this friendly waitress brought over a trucker to the counter where I was sitting. He said that he couldn't take me anywhere, but he offered to let me sack out in his truck's sleeping berth for a while.

"What a break that was! I slept into the evening until suddenly I was awakened by the trucker pounding on the door.

He startled me so much that I was barely able to crawl over to the cubicle's edge as he opened the door.

"He told me that truckers aren't supposed to pick up passengers because their insurance won't cover them. His suggestion was to start walking out of town on the main road. Even though it was getting dark and there wouldn't be much traffic, I'd just have to take my chances with hitchhiking.

"Before leaving, I went back into the restaurant and thanked that waitress for her kindness. She smiled and said that I was a grateful kid, not like so many of 'em. Then she motioned for me to wait a few moments.

"Back she came with two monstrous roast beef sandwiches. She also laid a couple of oranges on the counter and informed me that she was the night manager so these were also 'on the house.' I was to eat one of 'em, then take the other for the road. Nighttime had already moved in, so I'd be walking in the dark.

"As I began walking, I felt uneasy. I was unsure about what to do. Thankfully, the policeman, that waitress, the truck driver and you had been so kind to me. It was as if everybody I came into contact with was encouraging me to begin my new journey. I didn't have any other friends besides you people.

"In my whole life, I'd never visited with many folks except at church, but I was learning to trust Jesus even further. He was becoming my closest friend. Mister, I kept thinking that you had said not to look back. That was the message I had received from you!

"It seemed like ages before I walked far enough that the town was out of view. Gradually, its lights stopped blinking and faded out of sight. I was in total darkness and I could hardly see the edge of the highway. But I was picking up what you had said about being still and calm. As I looked up, I watched brilliant stars glimmer across the sky, and it was so much quieter. The last time I had seen stars so clear was when I had been out at sea on calm nights.

"This was a new kind of stillness, though, that I had never experienced while out at sea. At least back then I could hear the rhythm of waves splashing my boat. Being on ground was different. Nothing moved. The night had never seemed so quiet.

"Even though I was exhausted from walking into what seemed like nowhere in this desolate countryside, I felt a new feeling of relief. I realized that Jesus really was watching over me! The thought of the adventure I was walking into kept me going.

"Standing on the ground out there gave me a whole new feeling. My body seemed steadier and a peaceful feeling swept over me. I had forgotten how being peaceful felt.

"You had asked if I had guts. Well, I was being tested to see if I really had 'em. When I was out at sea during those storms, it had taken sheer guts just struggling to stay alive as my fishing boat often almost capsized. I just tried to survive.

"What I was experiencing out on the road took a different kind of guts, though. I was finding out for the first time in my life if I had what you talked about, mister.

"Suddenly, I stumbled badly and fell down, sprawled out right there on the highway. I stepped right into a pothole I hadn't seen on the edge of the road.

"For a few minutes I just laid there on the pavement, so stunned I was practically motionless. I finally gathered the courage to slowly start moving different parts of my body from my toes up to my head to see if I had hurt anything. Fortunately, I wasn't hurt, but I felt so alone.

"There I was, lying out there flat on my back on that dark highway in the middle of nowhere. A car or truck could have run over me, but there were no vehicles out there. Nothing had passed me in either direction for hours. It was so still.

"I seriously thought about turning back. I had walked and walked, probably many miles by now, but I was too tired to go back. But it would've been depressing to turn around. I'd have felt as if I'd a given up on myself! What also saved me was the other thing you had said on the pier that night. You had made a seemingly offhand comment, asking me what I had to go back to. That really stuck with me, 'cause the truth was, I didn't have anything to go back to.

"For my safety, I decided to get further off the road to rest on a nearby rock. Again, I looked up at those stars; those beautiful stars! My star gazing didn't last for long, though. I thought I saw a light on the horizon coming from the direction of town. As I looked again, sure enough, there it was. Something was coming closer. In fact, there were two sets of lights. Two vehicles were coming my way.

"I quickly got up, climbed off the rock, wiped off and straightened my blue jeans and stood at the edge of the highway. My arm, hand and thumb were outstretched, and I was eagerly hoping to be rescued.

"Two large trucks blared their horns as they sped by me, not even slowing down as they disappeared into the night.

"How depressing it was. But suddenly I remembered what you had said about praying to God. As I walked along, alone again, I kept crying out, praying to Jesus. The more frustrated I got, the louder I prayed!

"It was so dark. Doubts continued to creep in. I felt so abandoned, so alone. I got off the highway and sat down near another rock and crashed. It seemed like hours as I pondered what to do. The same episode repeated itself two more times. Nobody stopped. Other truckers just laid on their horns as they flew by. They probably thought I was some sort of animal.

"As I rested there on the rock, I was getting cold and started shivering badly. My teeth practically rattled. Suddenly, out of nowhere came another truck, whooshing by without seeing me. I was so depressed that I hadn't even bothered to get back up to hitchhike. There I was, resting only ten feet off the road, yet he hadn't seen me.

"As I gulped down my last roast beef sandwich and ate the remaining orange, an uncomfortable feeling swept over me. Had all of this been a bad mistake? I was scared, real scared. In fact, I had never been this scared in my life!

"The remoteness of that dark night was nerve-wracking! I didn't know what was ahead of me. The more I thought things over, though, I became even more determined to leave everything up to Jesus and not to look back! I kept promising myself that I'd keep trudging ahead.

"Another truck rushed by, horns blaring. Nothing. The same old result. Gradually, though, I was beginning not to care. To my surprise, I was even beginning to feel confident. Maybe I did have some guts after all! So far, nothing was going well for me, but at least I had done what you said to do.

"Yet another truck whooshed by, but this one seemed different. He didn't blare his horn. Even so, I felt dejected as he sped by.

"Suddenly, up about a hundred yards, I saw his brake lights go on. His rig screeched to a halt! The driver idled it, turned off the lights, jumped out and started hollering at me to hurry up and get in!

"If I would have been in an Olympic track meet that night, I would have won any dash! I ran a 'blue streak,' dashing down the middle of that highway faster than I had ever run!

"There he was, the same trucker who had let me rest in his rig back at the restaurant! He told me to duck down, 'cause he didn't want any other truckers to see me riding in his rig. It seemed like ages before he got going fast again. I counted him going through 18 gear shifts just getting back up to full speed.

"I must have looked awfully tired, because he told me to just sack out. That was the last thing I heard him say. I couldn't remember feeling so relaxed in my life!

"The sun was way up when I stirred, half awake, but enjoying a peaceful feeling that had come over me. I didn't know where we were headed, but I realized this was not going to be a scenic trip. Somehow, though, I didn't even care. It was such a relief to be inland!

"Hours passed and we both relaxed and began to talk. The trucker noticed I didn't have a wristwatch. I explained that none of us fishermen have watches, we just go by the sun and the moon. His response reminded me of the bold step I had just taken."

"Well, you're not a fisherman anymore," he said. "This is the real world out here, and you got to get a watch."

"I realized that even though I didn't know where I was going, this was the furthest I'd ever been away from my fishing boat. When he told me that we were headed to Pittsburgh, Pennsylvania, I didn't even know where that was.

"I confessed that I didn't know what I was going to do when we got there. But he had been working on that while I was sleeping and already had a plan. He had called his wife and asked if he could bring me home with him.

"At that point, I was completely bewildered, but somehow I trusted that man. Jesus was watching over me! And you, the policeman, the friendly waitress and now this trucker were all watching over me. All of you had been so kind to help me."

By this time, this phone call had my full attention. "Well, Franco, what finally happened to you?" I quickly asked.

Franco continued his story. "We took a long, tiresome, almost 30-hour journey. It seemed like forever that I was crumpled up in that front passenger seat, being forced to stay hunkered down and out of view.

"It was late at night when we finally trucked into a little town east of Pittsburgh. Although the night was at its darkest and dawn was approaching when we pulled up to his place, a huge crowd of church friends and neighbors gathered to welcome us. They just stood there, cheering and clapping!

"In fact, they woke up the whole neighborhood. The neighbors quickly put on clothes and rushed out into the street to see what all of the commotion was. I was completely surprised and dumbfounded! Even their church's pastor and his family were on hand to greet me.

"The trucker and his wife took me home. I was ushered into a guest room that was all fixed up just for me. To my surprise, the bed I was to sleep in even had sheets on it. I couldn't remember ever sleeping in a bed with sheets. That night, I got the best rest I've ever had in my life.

"The next Sunday, I went to church with the trucker and his family. Their pastor asked for a special collection to be made so members in the congregation could get me some clothes and other needed items. Folks went home and searched through their belongings that week. That following Sunday they brought back clothing, gloves, jackets, winter coats and more, all to be given to me.

"When I tried to tell them I didn't need a winter coat because it was summer, they laughed uncontrollably. The church folks said I would need one for sure because winters get pretty cold in Pittsburgh. They even said I would see frozen water. That was to be a new one for me 'cause the sea never froze.

"The trucker's family not only put me up at their place, but they let me stay there without having to pay rent. He talked to his boss and even got me a laborer's job unloading big rigs on the docks at the company's trucking warehouse.

"Gradually, it started to sink in that I was no longer a fisherman. I didn't miss my fishing boat or the harrowing, discouraging life that had gone along with it!

"Word was spreading around about the young 'un who had left the only life he had ever known way back in Maine. One evening, they interviewed me on one of Pittsburgh's main TV stations. Afterwards, people started calling in who were awed at my crude graphic art displays they had shown on TV.

"And it kept getting better. The state of Pennsylvania got involved and they made it possible for me to get my GED certificate 'cause I never graduated from high school.

"A vocational technical school let me attend there on reduced tuition with a hardship status. I worked at the trucker's warehouse in the evenings so I could pay my own way. I wanted no part of building up any debts.

"This past spring, I graduated from that technical school with honors in graphic design. For graduation, the trucker and his family bought me a real nice wristwatch! I wondered how they came up with that idea.

"Then I got a good job and even have a nice girlfriend. Who knows? We might even get married next year! She knows better than to ask if I ever want to take a trip to see the ocean, though. I suppose that someday I'll go back to see it. My girlfriend knows that I never want to leave shore again in my life. It was those terrible storms! I don't know how I survived them. It's just that I didn't know any other way of living.

"Mister, I needed to make this phone call to thank you. If it wouldn't have been for you, I'd have probably been dead by now, swept away at sea. I wanted to wait until I had graduated before calling you.

"Ever since I've entered my new life, I've kept looking at your business card. In fact, I've even memorized it. Even when I temporarily lived at that trucker's home, I stuck your card up on the bathroom mirror I used. Some folks asked what that card meant. I just smiled and said the man who gave it to me brought me closer to Jesus. He literally saved my life!

"My Bible and your business card are my most treasured possessions. Somehow, others seem to understand when I tell them my story.

"Looking back to that night I left my old life, it was so scary and frustrating out on the lonely highway! But I just kept walking, crying out to Jesus, praying, talking, beseeching Him the best I could. Each time it got more frustrating, I prayed out even louder than I had shouted out at sea.

"At first, I didn't think I had it in me, but I found out that I did! Jesus sure did answer my prayers. He became my closest friend. Every morning I say a prayer, asking Him to watch over you. Mister, you taught me the greatest lesson I've ever learned about life!"

After we hung up, I marveled at the amazing story I had just heard. Hearing the joy in his voice brought tears to my eyes as I realized what can happen if I just follow God's direction to be kind to a stranger. To this day, whenever I think about

Franco, I just shake my head in wonder. Our conversation on that pier had started out so simply and had lasted only a short time. But it brought lasting impact in Franco's life, and could affect the lives of his family for generations to come. As for me, I know this encounter has changed my life forever.

◆━━━━━━━━━◆

*Therefore, as we have opportunity,*
*let us do good to all...*
Galatians 6:10

*As we have the opportunity.* Those words really capture my attention – and my heart. I've learned to be looking for opportunities to bless someone. To do good to them.

Have I always acted this way? I must admit that I haven't. I've missed many opportunities that have come before me over the years. But God never wants us dwelling on our failures. He wants us to learn from our mistakes and press on. In fact, He will help us if we just give Him the chance.

That's what happened when I met Franco. I didn't know him or anything about him. But as I listened to him tell me his story back in Bar Harbor, I was also listening to God and asking what, if anything, I could do to help him. And that's when the answer came.

The next time you encounter someone who could clearly use some help, pause for a moment and listen. You just might hear a still, small voice rise up within you and show you the way that you could be an answer to someone's prayer.

*Kindness is a passport
that opens doors
and fashions friends.
It softens hearts
and molds relationships
that can last lifetimes.*

Joseph B. Wirthlin
Businessman

# 3

# EMILY

*Rewarded for my kindness – 60 years later.*

When I was still quite young, our family made what I thought was an exciting move from a large metropolitan city in Connecticut close to New York City, to a small sleepy town in Wisconsin. Moving into that town is something I will never forget, and to this day, I'm still a small-town kid at heart.

The sights and sounds of growing up in that town in the late 1940s still crowd my mind. I can close my eyes and hear the shrill sound of the paper mill whistle, the clickety-clack of the afternoon freight train hauling logs from up north, the ringing of the ice cream truck's bell and the creaking of the old gray wooden floors of our town's grocery store.

One of the most haunting sounds I remember, though, was the weak, discomforting whimper from a skinny, pigtailed kid in our first grade class. And was she ever skinny! One of my closest friends could put his forefinger and thumb around her upper arm and both of his fingers could touch each other.

Many of the neighborhood kids picked on her because she was so frail that she couldn't even muster a full cry. This girl, however, was one of the nicest, kindest people in our entire class. Her name was Emily.

Fortunately, my friends, Jimmy and Art, and I felt sorry for this fragile little girl. As classmates, we made a point to be-friend Emily and to play with her, especially when we played out on the playground at recess.

Miss Wydra, our first grade teacher, was a tall, pretty lady who had auburn hair and striking green eyes. She seemed to understand what was happening with Emily. On some mornings, she even allowed the four of us to play for a few minutes beyond the recess bell.

One day, Miss Wydra kindly let Emily and me push our desks together. As I look back, I now realize that Miss Wydra knew Emily needed all of the help she could get. Miss Wydra and my mother had something in common: both of them were re-markable women who taught us kids *how to be kind to one an-other.*

When school let out for the day, I often carried Emily's books home for her. She lived in the upstairs apartment of an old brick tenement house less than five blocks from where our family lived.

One day she invited me to come over to her apartment to play. I was stunned at the sight and the stench of the run-down place! It was only a small, three-room apartment where Emily and her brother Leonard lived with their folks.

There was a small kitchen that also served as a dining room and a small living room. The crude bedroom where Emily's folks slept had a sink and a toilet in its corner. The entire building where she lived was inadequate, being built way back before the turn of the twentieth century. The place was one of the oldest buildings in town, dating back to the late 1880s.

Emily told me that she slept on the kitchen floor, sprawled out on some rags she kept stashed between the stove and the ice-box. (They did not have a refrigerator.) She said that sometimes it got so cold at night that she had to drape the coat she wore to school over her as a blanket.

Emily was a grateful little girl. I think she appreciated the kindness that Jimmy, Art and I kept showing her out on the playground. She always said "thank you" for those small, kind gestures we made to her. One morning, as a token of appreciation, she brought an orange to school so we could share it at recess. (It would also help us disguise the horrible taste of those brownish-gray goiter pills we were required to take at the nurse's office in those days.)

Little did I know what a struggle it was for Emily to bring that orange to school, but I was about to find out.

When I saw her apartment and the conditions in which she lived, it became painfully clear that sharing that orange with me probably meant that Emily had gone to bed the previous night without much supper. I was dumbfounded that such poor folks lived only within blocks of our home.

Emily and I had so much fun playing together, that I became

accustomed to going over to her place. The kids at school gradually began to accept her, and Miss Wydra really encouraged us all by demonstrating her kind way. Slowly, Emily was gaining acceptance within our class.

When we reached second grade, to our surprise we found out that Miss Wydra would again be our teacher. It was somewhat common in those days for some children to have the same teacher for more than one grade.

As second grade proceeded, Emily became my closest friend. She was swift as lightning on the playground, and was often one of the first kids to be chosen when we sided-up to play baseball. She could really hit that ball!

Spring came and went and we were looking forward to spending a fun summer together in the park. The kids were already claiming they were almost third graders! There was even talk about a new swimming pool that was to be built in the park across from our house. But on a beautiful June day, something completely unforeseen happened!

When I went over to Emily's apartment to get her to play baseball with us, I knocked on the door and found that it was unlocked. That was strange. I shouted to see if anybody was at home. There was no answer! I climbed the old rickety, wooden stairway, gingerly stepping on each stair, as I always did, for fear it might collapse. To my horror, the place was empty. Emily was gone!

Almost before I knew it, more than 60 years – more than a half century – had passed. Many class reunions had come and gone, but Emily was the one person with whom I wished I could have kept in contact. Perhaps she wasn't even alive anymore. After all, some of our grade school companions had already passed away.

One day, I ran across a couple of old class pictures that showed us in first and second grade. There was Emily, wearing the same dress both years.

A few years ago, I decided to attempt to locate Emily and to find out whether she was still alive. One of my former classmates told me that he thought Emily's brother Leonard still lived in the town next to where we grew up. This tidbit of information at least gave me a place to start. My hopes were quickly dashed, though, when I found out that Leonard's telephone number had been disconnected.

At first, I had no further leads. However, one appeared when I found the telephone number of a person with the same name who was living way out in the country. Could this possibly be the same Leonard I had been trying to reach? I discovered that it was!

When Leonard and I talked on the phone, he couldn't remember me. (He had been much younger than Emily.) I found him to be quite distant. He surely didn't understand why I was trying to locate his sister and was unwilling to give out her unlisted phone number.

Finally in desperation, I gave him my name, address and phone number and asked if he could at least give this information to his sister. I hung up, massively frustrated that I couldn't accomplish more. Oh well, at least she was still alive.

Within five minutes, my phone rang. There even seemed to be

a *special ring* to the phone this time. When I answered (on the first ring), I heard an excited voice. No, it was a scream, a shriek! IT WAS EMILY!

Here, after all of those years, we had finally gotten back in touch with each other!

As we talked, I learned that she was married to an older man who was retired from farming. They were living out in the country in a rural area, west of the small town where we used to live.

It was so tempting to linger on the phone, to get caught up on 60 years of news. Instead, we decided to reunite. Emily and I made plans to meet in front of the old grocery store at a cross-road out in the country.

When the day came to reunite with her, I actually had butter-flies in my stomach. Finally I came to my senses and thought to myself, *Schiebs, this is ridiculous! You haven't had butterflies like this since you were back in high school getting ready to go to your junior prom.*

It was finally time. As I carefully and slowly pulled up, I parked across the street from the grocery store. THERE SHE WAS! I immediately recognized her. Even though she now had gray streaks in her hair, she was still the thin girl I remembered. I hardly had time to get out of the car before she was there. We just clung to each other.

As we walked across the street to her car, something amazing happened. We didn't realize it, but we had just walked across that street holding each other's hands.

Here were two adults carrying on as if they were kids. As we talked about it later, both of us agreed that it just seemed like the appropriate thing to do.

When we got back to Emily's house, a nifty surprise awaited me. Her kids ran up, hugged me and each simultaneously kissed me on my cheeks! Emily just stood there grinning, taking it all in.

One of her children told me this was the most excited they had ever seen their mother! For years, they had heard her talk about her closest friend way back when she was a little girl. They felt as if they had known me all along.

We had an enjoyable picnic outside and talked about the old days. Before I knew it, the sun was setting and it was time to go home.

We said our goodbyes, promising that we would never get out of touch again. That night I drove home, savoring one of the most fulfilling days of my life, and realizing that the result of kindness is truly never-ending.

◆—————————◆

> *But You are God,*
> *Ready to pardon,*
> *Gracious and merciful,*
> *Slow to anger,*
> *Abundant in kindness...*
> Nehemiah 9:17

Even when I was a kid, I knew that doing good and showing kindness was always the right thing to do. Oh, that's not to say that I didn't get in my share of trouble. But what I learned from listening to and watching my mother always came through. And she always gave credit to God.

As this passage says, God is *abundant in kindness.* Jesus was a perfect example of that. Wherever He went, and whomever He met, He recognized what was most needed by someone and went out of His way to be kind and meet their need.

Some people needed encouragement. Some people needed healing. Others needed to find the truth. And every time, Jesus gave them just what was needed.

As a Christian – a Christ-follower – I need to be doing the same things that Jesus did. He perfectly represented His Father to the world. We all should be demonstrating the love and kindness of God to everyone we meet. When you do that, not only will you make someone else's life better, but *you* will reap the rewards of kindness, too.

*A little thought
and a little kindness
are often worth more than
a great deal of money.*

John Ruskin
Writer, Artist

# 4

# VISITORS FROM THE RAILROAD TRACKS

*Mother always knew best.*

One day on my way to the federal courthouse in downtown Minneapolis, a man approached and asked me for some change. He was obviously much younger and physically more able-bodied than I was. Realizing I could not distinguish between a homeless person who was truly needy and someone who was just trying to make an easy buck, I didn't give him much.

As I thought about that encounter, I realized that times and titles have changed. Alcoholics used to be called drunks. Homeless people were labeled as bums. Perhaps it was my childhood idealism, but when I grew up, hoboes and other unfortunate folks, especially homeless combat veterans who lived by the railroad tracks, seemed to be more respectful of a balance in life. There was no such thing as welfare back in those days, and those folks knew that to survive, they had to give back some useful service in return for what they received.

When I was a boy in Port Edwards, Wisconsin, needy people knocked at our family's door, offering to do something for us like rake leaves, sweep our driveway or sharpen dull scissors, instead of merely asking for handouts. That was life in small towns close to busy railroad tracks.

Shortly after World War II in 1947, I was six years old. Our small town was in the middle of Wisconsin and fewer than 1,200 people lived there. The main industry in town consisted of a large paper mill that always bustled with activity. We lived only a block away from huge lumber yards that were supplied daily by three separate railroads.

Every afternoon, precisely at 12:58, I dashed out of our house and ran down to stand by the Chicago Northwestern railroad tracks to look northward up the tracks. I was eager to see the southbound train hauling logs from lumber camps up in northern Wisconsin.

Sure enough, at exactly 1:00 p.m. (I could set my watch by its arrival), I'd see the black, billowing puffs of smoke as the coal burning train engine rounded the bend. It was old number 1385. Those engineers actually got to know me as they whooshed past and waved.

However, I must admit that one time I got into big trouble with my parents when I held my younger sister Karen hostage as the huge engine sped by. The engineer blew side steam in her face! Even though it had cooled down by the time it hit her, she was frantic and ran home in tears to tell my folks.

Oh boy, was I in for it! I was grounded forever. In fact, I think

my sentence was just lifted late last week. I learned in no un-
certain terms that crime (and a big brother's joke) does not
pay.

In those days, my mother taught me a lesson about kindness
that I never forgot. She used to tell us children that Jesus always went out of His way to help downtrodden people. One
day her efforts were directed toward homeless folks who lived
in the wood yards where the three railroads converged.

While I was out playing, I streaked around the corner of the
house and ran right into someone's big, burly arms! There was
no time to scream before I saw my mother, who was standing
with this man and two of his friends.

You should have seen them. They weren't just dirty, all three
of them were filthy from head to toe and their clothes were in
shambles. One man had three front teeth missing. Another's
head was almost completely bald with just a scruffy rim of
gray hair. The third was so skinny that I was sure the snakes
in the rail yard thought he was one of their own.

The big, burly one greeted me. "We found out your name is
Bill when we heard your friends call out to you."

Then he said something that was quite startling to me. "By the
way, that's quite an underground fort you're building over by
the wood yards."

Up until then, I had mistakenly thought that my fort's location
was *my* secret.

These men were introduced as friends whom mother had
known for several years. Her statement confounded me. I had

never seen them or heard about them before. Why had those people decided to live like that? Where did they come from? My mind raced with unanswered questions.

Our neighbors knew that my mother had handy uses for discarded pots and pans. These odd pieces of cookware accumulated in her kitchen, then suddenly disappeared. Sometimes she would come home from the grocery store with unusual items such as canned potatoes. I could never figure out why she bought them because our family always had fresh potatoes, not canned. Like the cookware, one day they were here and the next, they were nowhere to be found.

Mother always told us she bought those potatoes and saved the pots and pans for useful purposes. It was only later that I found out she would give these items to the homeless men that would come to the door.

In those days, hoboes talked among themselves and chose the child they thought had been the friendliest while playing by the huge log piles along the railroad tracks down from the paper mill. They would follow that youngster home, carrying small chunks of coal that had fallen along the railroad tracks.

Those men knocked gently on the family's door, hoping to find parents who were as friendly as their child had been. If the men received a handout, they took their piece of coal and marked a slash on the curb in front of that particular house. That way, other homeless folks who were going by would know there was a friendly family living there and they might receive a handout as well. I used to see small pieces of coal lying in the streets, but never gave much thought as to where they had come from.

As time went on I felt easier about playing closer to the people who lived around the railroad yards. For a couple of years I had been using some of the small logs outside the paper mill as roofing for my fort. Whenever I went to pick out a log to use, I always wondered why the best logs were usually the easiest to remove from the piles. One of the men I bumped into that day told me the reason.

He told me that they wanted to help me with building my fort, but for them to carry logs to my "secret" fort location would have been too obvious. Instead, they helped me by re-arranging the piles to make the best logs the most accessible for me.

Our society has moved on. We have supposedly become more civilized. But I wonder if we haven't regressed from some of those old traditions where the haves and have-nots would show respect for each other and strike that delicate balance of life, where all would benefit.

One time after our friends left to wander back to the railroad tracks, I ran out into the street to see if there was a coal slash on the curb in front of our house. To my surprise and delight, I found *three slashes* on our curb that day!

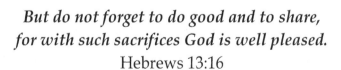

*But do not forget to do good and to share,*
*for with such sacrifices God is well pleased.*
Hebrews 13:16

The lessons I learned by interacting with those men from the rail yard have stayed with me all these years. The value of sharing. Treating others with respect. Helping those less fortunate. These were life-lessons that were passed on to me by my parents, and which I tried to share with my own children as they were growing up.

It wasn't by talking (or lecturing, as they might say), although we certainly had conversations about these important issues. But like my mother and father, I let my children watch me as I put into practice those things I felt were critical to living a godly life.

All of these are rooted and grounded in the Bible. Within the pages of God's Word, it talks about doing good to others more than 300 times. Some of the "others" it mentions are widows, orphans, the elderly, prisoners, the poor, the sick, the homeless, your neighbors, and more.

You probably know someone in one of these categories right now. Or, perhaps there was a time when you found yourself desperately in need of help from someone. The point is, no one should have to shoulder that kind of burden alone.

Maybe all you can do is offer a kind word. But that loving gesture may be just what that person needs in order to hold on until help arrives. We can all do something, and if you want to be a person who helps others, it won't be hard to find someone who needs exactly what you have – a willing and compassionate heart.

*An enemy to whom you show kindness becomes your friend.*

Saadi
Iranian Poet

# 5

# KINDNESS IN THE MIDST OF CHAOS

## *Following my grandpa's advice saved hundreds of lives.*

Before leaving for combat in Vietnam, I drove my parent's car from our home in Wisconsin Rapids to Appleton, Wisconsin, so I could visit my treasured grandpa who was then 91 years old. He was the only grandparent I had ever known.

As I pulled up to the curb, I couldn't help but notice some neighbors watering the flower beds in their front yard. As I got out of the car, all decked out in my Army dress greens as a junior officer, second lieutenant, their eyes were glued on me, following my every move as I resolutely strode up Grandpa's front walk. The inquisitive, piercing stares from his neighbors made me feel uneasy.

Somehow, I felt Grandpa knew that troubling times were on the horizon. Just as I had recently completed formal military training, hostilities in Vietnam began to escalate. For the first time in our nation's history, casualty figures had become a disturbing part of each evening's news. Ghastly combat scenes flashed into people's living rooms on nightly television coverage.

What I hadn't foreseen was that mounting combat casualties had become overwhelming. The army wasn't able to keep up with the delivery of the increasing volume of death notices within our division.

Out of desperation, the Department of Defense resorted to recruiting taxi cab drivers to hand-deliver death notices to the next of kin. This burden was to fall on their shoulders at all hours of the day or night.

Julie Moore, the wife of Lieutenant Colonel Hal Moore, watched these deliveries at Fort Benning, Georgia and went out of her way to contact and comfort the families who were receiving these notices. She recognized that this was a terrible way to deliver such devastating news. As a result of her persistent objections, within a few weeks, the Army changed its policy and required that only an officer and chaplain would be allowed to deliver death notices.

As I thought again about the blank stares from my grandpa's neighbors, could it be that they were wondering if the reason for my visit that morning was to deliver a heartbreaking death notice from the Department of the Army?

In many ways, I felt self-assured, perhaps even a bit cocky, as only a wet-behind-the-ears, runny-nosed, 24-year-old brat kid could feel. After all, I was a member of one of the most elite fighting units in the United States Army, a paratrooper in the airborne Rangers. At least, that's what our jumpmasters had led us to believe by telling us over and over again.

Was I invincible? Absolutely not!

As I strode up the sidewalk to Grandpa's front porch that morning, I felt uncharacteristically unsure of myself. Even though I had volunteered to serve in the paratroopers and Rangers, I kept thinking what a fine mess I'd gotten myself into.

Maybe my brash, youthful exuberance had been eroded by the astronomically high casualty rates, especially among airborne Rangers. (Years later, it would be revealed that young infantry rifle platoon leaders, like I was, suffered one of the highest mortality rates in Vietnam.) My snazzy appearance in a dashing paratrooper's uniform bedecked with a Ranger Tab on my left sleeve, and crisp, bloused pants tucked into spit-shined boots did nothing to reinforce my wavering confidence at a time like this.

That morning my confidence had been shaken by the horrifying accounts I heard of how combat carnage had decimated many Army units. In all honesty, I was scared; so scared that I actually felt numb inside and weak-kneed as I climbed the steps of Grandpa's tidy, shaded, front porch.

He was rocking back and forth in his favorite chair, eagerly awaiting my arrival. I had made a conscious effort to arrive early that morning while it was still fresh and cool, out of respect for Grandpa's waning energy level and heat tolerance.

It hadn't yet reached 10:00 in the morning, but already locusts were swarming in the trees above us. A sweltering, muggy, late July day was brewing.

Grandpa was looking forward to seeing me! Our relationship went way back to when I used to snuggle into his lap as he read my favorite bedtime stories. As he gingerly pried himself from his rocking chair to greet me, his eyes brightened. We were to share such a meaningful visit that morning.

Even in my excitement, a dismal feeling strangled my emotions. Would this be the last time I would ever see the only grandparent I had ever known? Though reluctant to admit it, I was bracing myself for the possibility of never returning from combat alive to see my family, my loved ones or my friends again.

After Grandpa and I finished visiting, he struggled to his feet, ready to offer a somber, but emotional, goodbye. Both of us realized the precious moments we had just spent together might well be our last time with each other this side of Paradise.

Just as I was going to do an about-face and leave, Grandpa clutched my forearm with both of his bony, weathered hands, calloused from years of manual labor in the paper mills. Did he have something profound to pass on to me?

In his wise but gentle tone, he counseled, "Now you remember, Billy, always, always be kind to the enemy prisoners you'll capture. God loves them just as much as He loves you!"

For a moment I just stood there, frozen in my boots. Stunned at the depth and sincerity of his advice, I was at a loss for words, and struggled unsuccessfully to choke back my flow of tears.

It was the fall of 1965. There I was, a young first lieutenant platoon leader, commanding a small infantry unit of 45 men as part of the Army's First Air Cavalry Division.

In the annals of military history, combat troops had never been deployed by helicopter before Vietnam. We were startled when we first heard the deafening roar of countless choppers (as we called them) with their turbine-driven blades whap-whap-whapping through the air. Our division had 457 choppers. I can't remember how many times we had to get into and out of those choppers.

We had been rapidly thrust into the thick of battle. Although relatively fresh into combat, my platoon had found themselves fighting for their very lives in extremely close quarters. What a bloody nightmare it had become – a virtual baptism under fire! Some units in our division had already become locked in fierce, pitched, hand-to-hand battle with a tenacious, well-armed, superbly trained, well-supplied, ferocious enemy. Bayonets on both sides had been bathed in blood!

Agonizingly intense, protracted fighting had left us utterly exhausted. We had already grown weary of fighting in the sweltering jungles of Vietnam.

Due to fighting tooth and nail at bayonet's length, our platoon had developed a seething hatred toward our enemy. If that wasn't enough, battle-hardened North Vietnamese Regulars (not Viet Cong) did not take prisoners. Any Americans captured were executed on the spot!

In less than two months of ferocious fighting, our platoon had already experienced an alarmingly high casualty rate and change of personnel. As their platoon leader, it had gotten to the point where I didn't have the foggiest idea as to who our new replacements were.

In desperation, I resorted to marking the sides of my men's helmets with zeroes for enlisted soldiers and triangles for my sergeants. This was a simplified means of identifying who was who; something I especially needed in the heat of battle.

We were nearing the onset of the rainy monsoon season, and my battle-weary men had been struggling just to stay alive. One evening, we had just entered the Ia Drang Valley in the far western mountainous region near the Cambodian border. Unfortunately, especially in that particular area, we had been "getting our clocks cleaned" at the hands of North Vietnamese Regulars.

Late that night, about 0200 hours (2:00 a.m.), our field radio barked. *Crackle . . . Pop . . . Crackle!* Amidst the static, a whispering voice was barely audible.

Our radios were lousy. In mountainous terrain, their transmission often couldn't even reach the length of six football fields. All voices coming over "the horn," as we called our radios, were usually garbled. On this particular night, this soldier's words were distorted at best.

Could it be our rifle company's executive officer (the second in command)? Whoever it was, it certainly was an urgent distress call, pleading for help. Although transmission was barely audible, a few jumbled words were still coming through.

Fortunately, we recognized that distinct command voice. Without a doubt, it was Paul. He was stranded far out behind enemy lines. Speaking in muffled tones so that he wouldn't give away his position, Paul told us he was in a desperate situation. His movement was being slowed down by two injured North Vietnamese prisoners. They were getting farther and farther behind our rifle company as we were moving through the jungle.

Our company commander was very concerned that we were going to lose our company's executive officer. He gathered the four platoon leaders and asked if one of us would venture out, way behind enemy lines, to rescue him. I volunteered to go get Paul because I was not about to let him down. He was my closest friend during combat and would have done the same for me no matter what the odds were.

Little did I know the hazards we would soon face. Venturing out into the jungle with only ten men and a machine gunner to help find him, was to prove to be extremely difficult. My specialized training and combat experience were surely being put to the test.

We instructed Paul to fire a shot in response to our radio signal. He was to do so until we could get a fix on his location. Then, we could quietly make our way through enemy territory to rescue him.

Each time he fired a shot, though, the whole jungle erupted with enemy gunfire! That quickly caused us to change our plan, and we told Paul *not* to fire again so he wouldn't give away his position. It was decided that we would fire two periodic rifle shots, and as a result, he was able to quietly guide us to his location by radio.

With each shot we fired, however, the enemy responded with gunfire of its own. It became apparent that we were surrounded by enemy forces!

On our way to rescue him, we practically bumped into two separate, roving enemy patrols. Our ten-man patrol missed them by less than 30 feet! As soon as we saw them, we had no option but to freeze in our tracks, otherwise, they would have easily detected us. None of us even dared crouch down or our movement would have been noticed. Our rescue mission was fraught with peril every step of the way.

After a couple of incredibly tense hours, we finally found Paul, his radioman and their two prisoners. They were plodding along a dry creek bed that had become an obstacle course of jagged rocks. His small party had been futilely attempting to make their way back to our lines. They were exhausted and at the point of collapse.

In the red glow of my flashlight (at night, this subdued glow could be seen for less than 50 feet), I could barely make out one of the barefoot prisoners. His feet were masses of bloody pulp! It was obvious this North Vietnamese prisoner would have great difficulty keeping up as we made our way back to our main unit. He could become our albatross!

For a fleeting moment, I hesitated. I had already witnessed so many of my good friends die at the savage hands of the North Vietnamese that I was seething with hatred toward this prisoner. In the throes of my dilemma, I wrongfully rationalized that one bullet would quickly resolve this problem!

Suddenly, my soul stirred, bringing to mind my grandfather's parting counsel regarding kindness to enemy prisoners. I abruptly came to my senses, recalling his apt advice, "Bill, just remember that God loves your enemies just as much as He loves you."

Without hesitating, I picked up this prisoner, carefully hoisted his pain-wracked body over my shoulder, and started carrying him toward our entrenched rifle company.

With my M-16 automatic rifle in my left hand, I balanced my prisoner with my other arm. He reeked of nuoc mam, the strong smelling and rancid fish sauce used in Vietnamese food. Since his tattered uniform bore no insignia, I had no way of knowing the rank of the prisoner slung over my shoulder. Only much later would I discover that information, but in a quite unexpected way.

Our trek began along the rugged creek bottom, and then led up through thick jungle. My small ten-man patrol had been isolated on its rescue mission for almost the entire night. Without a doubt, of all nights, this was the most terrifying one I had experienced in combat.

Stress and fatigue had worn me down. My body was near collapse and I was so tired that I questioned the reliability of my judgment. Was it affecting my combat awareness? The strain. The fatigue. I just didn't have much energy left.

As I struggled along, I realized my weighty responsibility of leadership in combat. Lives were in harm's way. This was the very time I desperately needed to lead our patrol back to safety and this wounded North Vietnamese prisoner slung over my shoulder like a hundred-pound sack of potatoes certainly wasn't helping.

To make matters worse, as I trudged along, I detected faint weeping. Had he misjudged us, thinking we were all ugly Americans? Did he fear he was to be shot on the spot, like the North Vietnamese treated our men who were taken prisoner?

Pretending not to hear him, I smugly thought I could successfully ignore him, but he began sobbing uncontrollably. Immediately, I became petrified! His sobs could betray our position. Instinctively, I gave him a slight squeeze, a nudge of reassurance.

Then, to my surprise and displeasure, I realized he began kissing me on the back of my neck! I was utterly embarrassed. Combat was bad enough. No way did I dare divulge this incident to anybody else in my platoon. It was to be almost 30 years before I could muster enough courage to admit what happened that night.

Finally, hours later, after a stealthy trek through dense mountainous jungle, our rescue patrol stumbled into our main unit's protective perimeter. Once securely inside, we turned our prisoners over to the medics.

It was over. I was so drained that I collapsed on the rocky ground and for a few minutes, just laid there motionless. My company commander just shook his head in bewilderment as he looked at me, lamenting that I had been forced to carry this wounded prisoner for over three miles.

Surprisingly, the spirit of this small act of kindness spread like wildfire throughout our unit. Other men under my command were touched by the prisoner's medical condition. One of our medics went out of his way to give his bloody feet a healthy dose of antibiotic salve to ward off infection. I took off my own backpack, cut it in half and asked one of our machine gunners to fashion my prisoner some makeshift boots.

After we turned him over to our division headquarters for interrogation, I thought I would never see this prisoner again. Word sifted down to us that this North Vietnamese soldier had become intensely hostile, which was understandable with enemy prisoners. Much to my astonishment, he said he wouldn't talk to anybody except the tall one who had carried him to safety.

Consequently, they summoned me up to battalion headquarters. That was fine with me. At least I could get out of being shot at for an hour or two.

When I reached headquarters, I was brought to my prisoner. This time, though, this hostile North Vietnamese soldier seemed hesitant to talk, even to me. At first, I wondered if there was any point in trying. I doubted if there was any way to soften his hardened attitude.

What could I possibly do to ease his hostility?

In an attempt to overcome his hesitancy, I cautiously unsheathed my bayonet and began carving a rough outline of the United States in the dirt. I indicated where Wisconsin was, and then made a gesture toward myself. Through our battalion's interpreter, I attempted to explain where my home was. We were instantly met with a steely glare from this North Vietnamese P.O.W. It seemed futile.

For the life of me, I was stymied. I didn't know what to do.

Then, a most unlikely idea came to mind. I decided to gamble on how this prisoner might react, being surrounded by his captors, and wondered if he would try to make a last desperate attempt to retaliate against us.

Nevertheless, I chanced it and requested that the prisoner's handcuffs be unlocked and removed.

After we took off his handcuffs, he gingerly massaged his sore wrists. With my bayonet I drew a likeness of North and South Vietnam in the dirt. Then, I deliberately turned my bayonet over to him, giving him the handle and leaving the point of the bayonet facing me.

The men surrounding us gasped! Immediately they switched their weapons on to full automatic as they kept their watchful eyes glued on this prisoner. If this man would have made one threatening gesture, his body would have been splattered all over the place by hundreds of rounds of bullets.

Through the interpreter, I made another attempt to counter his hostility, asking him to point out where his home was on the map.

His response threw us off-guard. To everybody's surprise, our prisoner started smiling. Was his heart of granite finally softening? Wonder of all wonders, he had broken out in a toothless grin.

Perhaps he respected me for having the courage to turn my razor-sharp bayonet over to him. Here we were, as adversaries, having found a subject near and dear to every soldier's heart: our hometowns and family.

We began visiting with each other, exchanging locations and sharing about our families. Back home in the rice paddies of communist North Vietnam, he had a wife and two daughters. Halfway around the globe, near the Wisconsin cranberry bogs in capitalistic America, I had a younger sister and an older brother. There was no escaping that we both missed our families.

To our utter surprise, all of us were astonished when we learned he was a sergeant-major, the highest-ranking North Vietnamese captured thus far in the war. He proceeded to divulge crucial information that helped us get a fix on the whereabouts of the North Vietnamese units opposing us. He even went as far as disclosing the enemy's battle plan.

To this day, I think it was because of how kind we had been to him. Otherwise, I don't think he would have released the information he gave us. His revelations turned out to be tremendously useful, especially since our units were getting decimated. His accurate disclosure of enemy troop tactics, strength and location possibly saved hundreds of American lives!

Just think, a thoughtful act of kindness toward a wounded prisoner reaped huge rewards, thanks to my grandfather's heartfelt advice. As a result, fewer American boys would be shipped home in flag-draped caskets. What a reward for a simple act of kindness!

Though I went through a lot in Vietnam and have long ago readjusted to civilian life, combat memories remain firmly embedded within my mind.

As I reflect on my grandfather's advice and spiritual wisdom, I now realize it was not only helpful in combat, it is just as helpful in our daily lives. God lovingly watches over *all* of us! That consolation gives me strength to go forth with my life. Even today when I encounter a difficult person, I pause and remember: *Bill, be patient. Just remember that God loves them just as much as He loves you!*

◆――――――――――◆

*But love your enemies, do good, and lend, hoping for nothing in return; and your reward will be great, and you will be sons of the Most High. For He is kind to the unthankful and evil.*
Luke 6:35

Unless you have been to war, I think it's a pretty safe bet to say that you probably don't have an enemy that is actually trying to kill you, as I did in Vietnam. But that is exactly what Jesus was facing when He told His followers to love their enemies.

Jesus knew what it was like to have people who hated Him. He knew what it was like to have people speaking evil of Him wherever He went. And He knew how His time on earth was going to end – by sacrificing His life for the very people who stood against Him.

How about you? Is there someone from your past who has hurt you? Are you dealing with a person now who seems to go out of their way to make your life miserable? There might be people who simply rub you the wrong way or others who are just out-and-out mean.

Do you know what Jesus would say to you? Love them. Forgive them. Be kind to them. If you live your life like that, you will find that a sense of joy and peace will fill your life. For you will not only be showing God's love for others, but you will be portraying the same love and kindness that God has for you.

*There are realities we all share, regardless of our nationality, language, or individual tastes.*
*As we need food, so do we need emotional nourishment: Love, kindness, appreciation, and support from others.*

J. Donald Walters
Author

# 6

# CHRISTMAS EVE
# IN A BAMBOO PATCH

*Trapped behind enemy lines,
caring for one another
brings an unexpected result.*

Volumes have been written about the pros and cons of the United States' involvement in Vietnam. Few issues have divided our country as much since America's Civil War. Even the soldiers themselves would discuss, and often argue, about the value of the war.

Little did I know that less than a year after I left combat, I would be arrested and reprimanded for speaking out against our nation's involvement in Vietnam. Although I have always considered myself a patriotic American, after fighting over there and seeing the tactics that were used, I questioned our nation's commitment to the war.

But on one night, deep in the jungles of Vietnam, there was no discussion about politics. The men in my infantry rifle platoon were only serving our country. We were just trying to survive.

In spite of the differences in the racial and social backgrounds among these men, it was their kindness and concern for each other on a remote mountain hilltop that turned an extremely dangerous situation into one of gratitude and joy.

Our platoon's 1965 Christmas Eve in Vietnam started out to be the most dismal night any of us had ever experienced. We were supposed to have 45 men in the infantry rifle platoon I commanded (although we were seldom up to full-strength). Due to no fault of our own, we became isolated behind enemy lines that Christmas Eve, and were forced to make-do and fend for ourselves.

As a means of introduction, perhaps I should share with you what a bunch of questionable characters I commanded in my platoon. (I was probably the most questionable one of all.)

Some of the soldiers in my platoon were hardened criminals, including felons and murderers. Many of them had seemingly come from a different planet. They had grown up in some of the worst conditions imaginable. The places they called home in the 1960s were mostly filthy, rundown, crime-ridden neighborhoods in cities such as Chicago, New York City or Detroit. Few outsiders dared venture into the places where these men played as children, where back alleys weren't even safe in the daytime.

The lion's share of these men grew up being involved with vicious gangs. During their critical, habit-forming teen years, they had learned that survival-of-the-fittest ruled. They were forced to hang out with their peers in back alleys, rather than to be stranded in the no man's land of the ghettos. Each was forced to become a gang member for his very survival. The only way of life they knew was trying to eke out an existence in rundown neighborhoods that resembled combat zones.

Nearly 85% of my men were minorities. (The Armed Forces had just implemented racial integration less than two months before I entered active duty.) Vietnam wasn't much of an escape for these soldiers. For most of their years, each of these men had been fighting. They had merely emerged from one battle zone at home, only to be thrust into much worse conditions half-a-world away.

When I first went into the Army, many judges had been handing down sentencing options to convicted, hardened criminals. In lieu of long-term prison sentences, countless felons were forced to choose between rotting behind prison bars or dodging bullets as front-line infantrymen in Vietnam. Given such a forlorn choice, many of these convicts chose to pack weapons in the bush.

It didn't take long to see how this policy impacted our platoon. Matters came unglued in base camp right from the start. Three men under my command (two whites, one minority) committed cold-blooded murder of their fellow soldiers. For the safety of other soldiers, I was forced to physically disarm those men on my own.

From the mayhem I have just described, one would think these men were just a bunch of dangerous thugs. Wrong! Those infantrymen exhibited crafty, get-it-done ingenuity, especially under strenuous combat conditions. Despite their dubious past, surprisingly, my delinquents turned out to be terrific soldiers. From the moment we became locked in combat, they proved to be superb fighters. One couldn't have known a more capable, more courageous bunch of infantrymen.

To this day, I have the fondest memories of those unruly men. I have never felt closer to a more superb bunch of men than the scruffy soldiers in my platoon who fought by my side throughout those horrific firefights. In spite of their homicidal behavior, I feel privileged to have served with them.

My men knew I painstakingly watched out for them, putting their welfare ahead of mine. I made sure they received the first distributions of ammo, food, clothing and mail. In turn, the soldiers under my command watched over me whenever and however they could. It even got to the point where they fondly called me their Plat Daddy. (Plat is short for platoon.)

All of this set the tone for a Christmas Eve that would become indelibly etched in our platoon members' minds.

The small platoon I commanded was fighting in a remote mountainous region of the central highlands in Vietnam. Our infantry company was comprised of 186 men and was part of the Army's First Air Cavalry Division.

Earlier that Christmas Eve morning, helicopters had hovered over the tree tops as we jumped out and slid down cliff-rappelling ropes to the ground. The problem was, they had mistakenly dropped us off in the wrong location. Thanks to our chopper pilot's navigational oversight, we found ourselves 15 clicks off-target. (On our combat maps, a click was 1,000 meters.) We were nearly ten miles away from where we were supposed to be picked up and flown back to our main base camp that evening. There we were, stranded in remote, heavily mountainous terrain. It was a classic foul up.

A new departure order was issued to our stranded platoon. If we could make it back those 15 clicks to the intended map co-ordinates by 4:00 that afternoon, we would be air-lifted by chopper back to the relative safety of our base camp. Each platoon member could then relax and enjoy some security and a special turkey dinner for Christmas Eve.

Hooray! That would mean no C-rations for Christmas. (I say "yuck" to them.) Anytime we could get away from eating that so-called food in a can was a reason to celebrate. When my C-ration cans were dated 1947 (18 years prior), I knew I was in deep doo-doo!

Traveling ten miles over rugged terrain in just a few hours would require us to force-march, which meant we would hardly be able to take a break. Could we do it? Should we do it? That morning, I deferred the decision to my sergeants. Those older, grizzled combat veterans unanimously decided we should "throw caution to the wind" and attempt to move this long distance by foot in broad daylight to our new pick-up location.

Though our men were disheartened at the outset, these fugitives were real pieces of work. Not only were they extremely tenacious, it didn't take them long to get over their disappointment at the way our original mission had been botched-up. Their new-found optimism spread like wildfire, boosting our morale.

Suddenly, though, one of our men began complaining of dizziness due to dehydration. Temperatures had already reached a stifling, muggy, 97 degrees Fahrenheit by middle morning. (One man's mother had sent him a small outdoor thermometer. Mothers do kind things like that, you know.)

Our day had hardly begun. If this soldier collapsed, our hopes of reaching the pick-up zone in time to be airlifted back to our base camp would be flushed down the drain. Fortunately, just moments later, we stumbled upon a small, meandering brook that wasn't on our maps. I gave out the order to halt.

Some of my soldiers, including Sweetheart, Dreamer, Doubter, Razor, Pack Rat, Jimbo, Baiter, Master Whittler and Quiet One, set up a makeshift bucket brigade. (We had come up with nicknames for each other to retain some semblance of sanity.) Each of us paired off in teams of two and relayed water from the stream down below up a steep hill to our men.

Dreamer had just scarfed down his last remaining can of C-rations. He ingeniously improvised a makeshift funnel by gouging a small hole in the empty can with his bayonet so we could refill our canteens. Each two man team took turns straining the brook's water through our t-shirts into the other man's helmet (or "steel pot" as we called them). We then carefully poured that precious water from our helmet into one of seven canteens each of us carried.

Unfortunately, all water in Vietnam had to be purified, whether it was from brooks, streams or rice paddies. Not in your wildest, most vivid imagination, can you possibly comprehend *what* and *who* goes to the bathroom in *any* water in Vietnam. I'm sure there were bathrooms over there, but I never saw one.

"Yuk! This coffee tastes lousy!" Whenever we made coffee in the field, we voiced our daily complaint about such a taste-tempting (I should say taste-torturing) drink.

Blame it on Pack Rat. You should have seen this guy. His gear and all of the gizmos he dragged along made him look like a messy hobo with his own hardware store. We teased him, informing our junk collector that we could get most anything from him except a bathtub or an air conditioner.

On one previous occasion when we were greenhorns, unseasoned to combat, Pack Rat had chimed in, "You sissies knock it off! Quit bellyaching about your tasty coffee! All of you have sisters, wives, mothers, grandmothers, daughters and girlfriends back home. Write to 'em. Have them send you packets of pre-sweetened grape Kool-Aid. Dump a packet into each cup of your brew to dilute the terrible taste."

As I hesitantly dumped Pack Rat's savory ingredients into my canteen cup of cold water, it brimmed with C-ration instant coffee. We could never stop long enough to make fires to heat our chow or the North Vietnamese would find our position and begin mortaring us. The best we could manage was to concoct COLD coffee.

We had to stir the makeshift coffee brew with our fingers. When I took my finger out and looked at it, I noticed brown specks from powdered coffee, purple specks from Kool-Aid, white specks from Halazone water purification tablets and strange-colored specks from God-only-knows-what other crud from the stream.

At least with our canteens filled, we felt better with our new supply of water. Feeling a bit more hydrated, we were ready to resume our arduous trek. I mumbled to myself, "If I ever live to make it outta this dive alive, I'm never going to drink another cup of coffee again." (To this day, I don't drink coffee.)

My men wholeheartedly agreed that we would hoof it through the dense mountainous terrain and open fields. We were determined to do *anything* to complete our timed trek.

That day, we drove ourselves to the point of exhaustion, running for miles wherever the jungle and ravines were passable. We ran around bushes, through grassy fields, and went up, down and around hills. We waded through swamps under dense tree foliage and warily crossed clearings where the platoon was the most exposed and vulnerable. Instead of taking rest breaks, my men doggedly decided to furiously push on.

We finally reached our new pick-up location at 4:15 p.m., only 15 minutes late. When we arrived, our orders were to radio to base camp and our platoon would be air-lifted back to relative safety.

Even though the men were utterly exhausted, you should have seen the looks of eagerness on their faces. We had run and hacked our way, practically nonstop, over ten miles, all while lugging machine guns, rifles and full combat gear. (Guess who took his turn with lugging one of our machine guns?)

Jimbo, our radioman, practically gagged as he quickly forced down his last remaining can of C-rations. We anxiously waited while he made our expected radio call.

There's no way I can adequately describe how demoralized we felt when a squawk came over the radio with ominous news.

We had missed our deadline by 15 minutes. Only 15 minutes? Here we were, listening to some rear echelon-type back within the secure confines of division headquarters, callously informing us that it wouldn't be possible to airlift our platoon back to camp as planned that evening. They were having their own merry old time back there. We would have to make-do and fend for ourselves.

Pangs of happier holidays of the past overwhelmed us. My memories of being raised in a close family that had festive Christmas Eves came back to haunt me. Now, we had no church service to attend, no Christmas carols to sing, no Christmas cards to read, no decorative Christmas tree or festive lighting, no presents (that we used to eagerly open), and no yummy Christmas Eve dinner. We certainly didn't have any holiday music.

Most of our C-rations had already been gobbled up. It was almost evening. Our platoon had been trudging through practically impassable mazes of jungle while sweating in tropical heat and humidity all day. By now, every man was exhausted, grubby, thirsty and hungry. Oh, we were *so hungry!*

Discouragement began to set in. Jimbo disgustedly kicked his empty C-ration can into the bush. We just stood there, motionless, awaiting a fate that should not befall any infantry soldier.

As for me, I was utterly frustrated! How could I possibly cheer up my men? Where could we hunker down to get protection for the night? I was overwhelmed.

Thankfully, within only a few seconds, Sweetheart came up with a flash of inspiration. He had spied a heavily wooded hill of spiny bamboo growth looming above the underbrush. Jungle bamboo is quite different from smooth bamboo fishing rods with which most of us are familiar. Horizontal, sharp barbs protrude from main limbs, much like barbed wire. If barely pricked by bamboo, one's skin immediately festers. Wild bamboo shoots grow so close together that cats can hardly wriggle their way through it.

This hill, tangled with the barbs of wild bamboo, was the safest place where we could set up a decent defensive barrier to protect us in case of an ambush.

As we hacked our way up through that mess of vegetation, it proved to be a formidable task. Even our strongest men with the sharpest machetes were challenged as they tunneled up through that nearly impassable snarl of growth. The musky scent of decaying bamboo permeated the air.

It took us almost two hours to chop through that maze of bamboo toward the summit of the hill. When we reached the top, all of us were exhausted and we collapsed in our tracks! Nobody could even summon the energy to dig protective foxholes. But we still needed to form our defensive perimeter.

Our men were only beginning to recuperate when Razor came up with a creative idea to temporarily fortify our position until we could dig in. He suggested placing an M-60 machine gun on the hill's crest, at the entrance of our narrow access tunnel. If the North Vietnamese tried to attack us that night, they'd have to crawl up through murderous machine gun fire!

Using protective cover (in this case, bamboo) when choosing where to place the machine gun was a classic example of the clever lessons my men had learned while fighting for their lives in the ghettos.

We had just managed to scale one of the steepest and most rugged hilltops in Vietnam's central mountainous highlands. And that was accomplished following a harrowing, ten-mile march. Our exhaustion was further complicated by the darkness that was quickly coming upon us.

Mist and fog had already formed, shrouding the valley below. Rapidly plummeting evening temperatures began chilling us to the bone. The oncoming coolness made everyone begin to shiver, and our struggles to stay warm were useless. Temperatures were to plummet to 55 degrees Fahrenheit that night. Something had to be done to warm us up.

Again, my men started complaining. Leave it up to Quiet One to come up with an ingenious idea to keep us warm. Why not build campfires? Surprisingly, his idea invigorated us!

Breaking a steadfast rule that strictly forbade open fires in combat, as darkness and chill set in, each of us mustered enough strength to dig shallow foxholes around makeshift fire pits. Defying rules of combat field operations, we lit our fires and clustered around them for warmth.

Wouldn't you know it, Doubter was skeptical. What else was new? As usual, he questioned the wisdom of standing in front of our fires. What he failed to realize was that nobody could detect our position up through that maze of bamboo.

As a Christian, I rationalized that if we got hit for preparing fires up on the top of that hill, it would "be a good way to go!" Doubter didn't challenge me any further.

As we stood in a circle in front of our fires, I encouraged my men to pray or meditate in their own way. Each of us attempted to relax and enjoy the unnerving calm we found ourselves in, far away from the base camp Christmas commotion.

We finally found enough energy to dig in and make our preparations for the night. I felt a bit unsure at first, as I didn't know how they would respond if I told them about the Christmas Eve I envisioned for them. I thought they might puke if I suggested they sing Christmas carols.

Each soldier hunkered down for what promised to be a long, agonizing, dismal night. Amidst the rank smell of decaying vegetation, I sprawled out, uncomfortably wriggling into my too-small foxhole, fully expecting a bummer of a Christmas Eve.

It was late, and that night was the darkest, clearest evening I remembered while fighting in Vietnam. Looking up at the awesome universe from my foxhole, I gazed in awe at millions of twinkling bright stars contrasted against an endless canopy of jet-black sky.

In the midst of those stars, I was able to make out the North Star and the Big Dipper. *If I would have been back home in the United States,* I thought, *I could have glanced up and seen those same stars.* For some unknown reason, though, they seemed even more brilliant here, half way around the world.

This was that special time of year when we celebrated the birth of our Savior, Jesus Christ. Those of us who were Christians didn't need a further reason to thrust ourselves into the true spirit of Christmas.

Each of us contemplated getting along without items traditionally associated with our normal Christmases. That night, we had stripped our festivity down to its bare essentials. There we were – stranded – but we Christians were warmed by the assurance that Jesus was right there with us, dwelling within our hearts.

As I gazed up at those bright stars, I thought about those three Wise Men who came to see the Baby Jesus. They didn't come to *get* gifts, they came to *give* gifts! Giving and paying homage was what their pilgrimage was all about. Honoring this long-awaited birth of our Savior was what really mattered. Jesus had come down to earth as a mere human being. He, God Himself, was to sacrifice His own life, to *give* His life for us in order to save us.

The silence was broken only by an occasional crackling of coals in the fire pits and the low mutter of men whispering to their buddies. Apparently, no fighting was occurring within our earshot. Then it started!

Out of the darkness a resounding baritone voice began singing *Silent Night*. For a fleeting moment, I just crouched there in my foxhole, bewildered. My platoon wasn't a group of singers. These men were a motley bunch, most of whom were downright thugs. To my utter surprise, our whole platoon then started joining in. Gradually, this rag-tag bunch began to sing louder and with enthusiasm!

Is it possible that music had been grafted into the hearts of even my most hardened platoon members? Not only did these hooligans get excited about being able to prepare fires (a rarity in combat), but how they could sing! Their harmony was breathtaking.

Each infantryman's feel for music, its rhythm and its harmony, seemed to come naturally. Some of my men even broke out into four-part harmony. For the life of me, I had no idea I was commanding a potential choral group.

Their beautiful singing took away the apprehension I had felt earlier about finding some way to provide them with a way to celebrate Christmas Eve while we were stranded far behind enemy lines.

Later that evening, I made my rounds from fire to fire, which by then had died down to glowing orange coals. Without exception, each of my men was lying on his stomach, face in hands, with tears streaming down his cheeks. This was indeed a fitting remembrance of the evening when Jesus Christ, our Savior, was born.

The next morning, when choppers finally lifted us back to base camp, their crews were dumbfounded at how surprisingly calm, relaxed, and contented my men were. Our platoon had made the most of what could have been a dismal Christmas experience.

Sadly, most of those same men didn't even survive another two months. They had barely lived long enough to usher in the New Year of 1966.

Our unit repeatedly kept running into fierce North Vietnamese resistance. The enemy really ripped our platoon to shreds! Very few of my men who celebrated their Christmas Eve in that bamboo patch managed to survive their combat tour of duty in Vietnam. As for me, I was exceedingly fortunate to have gotten out alive.

That Christmas Eve occurred many years ago. For years afterward, I wondered if any of the other survivors remembered the unforgettable evening we spent together up in that bamboo patch.

My answer finally came, but only years later when two grizzled survivors from our platoon drove halfway across the country from West Virginia and Ohio to visit me. We had heartfelt memories to share. Unexpectedly, as we talked, the three of us broke down and started sobbing! Each of us had seriously thought we'd never live to break bread together again.

To my surprise, they remembered that very touching evening on the hilltop in Vietnam. Our eyes moistened again as we recalled that Christmas Eve and the way every soldier had gone the extra mile to help and encourage each other throughout that difficult day. I had mistakenly thought that nobody else would remember that evening so long ago. They were to prove me wrong.

Both of them looked at me and asked, "Do you remember the Christmas Eve we spent in that bamboo patch? That was our most meaningful Christmas Eve ever!"

*Two are better than one,*
*Because they have a good reward for their labor.*
*For if they fall, one will lift up his companion.*
*But woe to him who is alone when he falls,*
*For he has no one to help him up.*
Ecclesiastes 4:9-10

Even though my playing days have long ago passed me by, I've always been a sports fan. I remember sitting on the sidelines of many games as my children and now my grandchildren were growing up.

"You can do it!" "Keep it up!" "Good shot!"

These shouts of encouragement echoed from the stands as parents and friends rallied in support of the players on the field.

For me, combat was the ultimate team effort. Each of us had to look out for the other soldiers in our squad, knowing that if one of us failed, it could impact everyone else in the worst way imaginable. We may have been very different from one another, but that didn't matter. What mattered was that we were a team with a job to do, and we had to work together to successfully (and safely) reach our objective.

Life is like that. Trying to go it alone as you deal with all that life throws at you is difficult and discouraging at best. No one wants to fail at life. We all need encouragement. So if you see a friend who seems down, be an encourager. We all need help from time to time. So if someone around you is struggling, be a helper.

Another passage in the Bible tells us, "With the same measure you use, it will be measured back to you." Don't hold back. Friends helping friends is a pattern of living that leads to success for everyone.

*It's not our job to play judge and jury, to determine who is worthy of our kindness and who is not. We just need to be kind, unconditionally and without ulterior motive, even, or rather, especially, when we'd prefer not to be.*

Josh Radnor
Actor

# 7

# BULLY BOY

*Surprising A Bully From My Past.*

When I was a youngster, I was a fragile, sickly kid. Although I was only four years old, I vividly remember being so clumsy that I tipped over a hot water steamer, scalding my back. To this day, I have little to no feeling over part of my back.

As I look back on my life, I now realize that I was doing clumsy things, even when I was barely four years old. To this day, I wonder when I actually began showing the first symptoms of having MS (multiple sclerosis).

As I entered fourth grade, I was one of the shortest boys in my class. Because of my frailty, I found myself playing out in the fields instead of participating in organized sports. It wasn't long before several classmates started questioning why I was always falling down. By the time I had entered high school, I had taken so many falls that I had broken my right wrist seven times and my left wrist two times.

Since I was so small, I didn't realize it but I was wide open to be bullied.

In our small school, Tommy and Dicky were well known as the town's bully and his sidekick. Tommy was not only three grades ahead, but he towered almost two feet over me. He had a twin brother, Carl, who just happened to be one of my closest buddies, but he was quite distant from his brother. As I think back, I don't remember the two of them ever getting along very well with each other.

One day I had my first encounter with Tommy and Dicky as I was walking home from school. Just as I walked past a back alley, those two ambushed me! Dicky idly stood by as Tommy beat the tar out of me. He even kicked me in the back as I was lying helpless on the ground. By the time he was finished, I limped home with a bloody lip and nose. My eye was bashed enough that, shortly thereafter, it turned black and blue. Tommy's last words were, "If you tell anybody who did this to you, I'll do it again!"

Nobody could keep a secret from my mother, though. She knew well what was going on. I'm sure she talked with our principal, but to my knowledge, nothing was ever done about the incident.

For two years, I was so scared that each day I took different routes walking home from school. At school, I shied away from Tommy, although I wasn't scared of Dicky because he was a short, pudgy kid who lived on a farm west of town.

One day, Dicky was fatally injured in his farmyard when he

foolishly attempted to pluck a piece of corn from an auger, which I later found out is one of the most dangerous pieces of farm equipment. That auger ripped off his arm. Since nobody could hear him scream, Dicky bled to death before his mother finally rushed up in horror. To my knowledge, he had been Tommy's only friend.

By the time I had reached sixth grade, I was growing so fast that our town doctor remarked, "Bill, your legs are hurting so badly because one bone is growing more rapidly than the other. Nothing to worry about. You'll outgrow your pain."

When I entered high school, I had become one of the tallest boys in my class. Now, I towered seven inches over Tommy. His bullying ceased. We just ignored each other.

My emotional scars, however, still lingered.

After I finished college, my life progressed on a different path than any of my friends had taken. I had gone into the Army, volunteered for the Rangers, and became a paratrooper. Combat was a hideous experience for me. Our unit got chopped up so badly that I thought I'd never live to see my hometown again.

When I finally did return home, my treasured friend, Carl, sensed I was having difficulties readjusting to civilian life. He stepped right up to the plate, making me feel welcomed and encouraged just when I needed it most.

He invited me and ten of our friends to a nearby steak house for a makeshift class reunion. A few days before we were to gather, though, I was a bit astonished when Carl asked me to take a drive out in the country so just the two of us could visit.

We both wanted to get caught up on where our lives were leading.

To my utter surprise, Carl brought up a painful topic: the time when Tommy bullied me. I muttered, "Carl, you really know how to hurt a guy, don't you?"

Carl was not to be swayed. He remarked, "Bill, you don't know this, but Tommy has fallen on desperate times. He's practically destitute. My brother is known so well in town as our school's bully that nobody wants to take a chance by hiring him. To make matters worse, I don't think he has a friend in the world.

"For the life of me, I don't know how he can even exist. For years he's lived at home, but our folks are getting along in life now. Both of them are already in their late 80s. When they pass on, where will Tommy go? Where will he live? How can he take care of himself? The people in town know that he at least cares for our folks, but that's not going to last forever."

"Well, I've got the craziest idea, Carl," I said. "Hear me out before you say no to me. Let's invite Tommy to dinner with us."

You should have seen the look on Carl's face. He just shook his head. "Bill, you're absolutely nuts. I never knew you to be so crazy. How in the world could we possibly get anybody else to come to dinner if Tommy is with us?"

"Doggone it, Carl, now hear me out on this. I think we could pull it off! Let's not tell anybody else that Tommy is coming to dinner until we get there. You walk in last with your brother. Since everybody else will be there, they'll just have to stay."

"You know what, Bill?" asked Carl. "Tommy is so desperate for attention from anybody else that I'd eat my shirt if he didn't accept my invitation. I'll set it up by telling him you don't even know I'm going to bring him to be with us for the evening."

My treasured friend had almost jumped out of the car when I first mentioned my idea, but as we talked, he grew more excited. Now he looked at me with piercing eyes. "Bill, this is a great idea. What do we have to lose?"

The evening finally arrived. I was already in the room chatting with my old schoolmates. Last of all, in walked Carl, accompanied by his brother Tommy. Nobody even had a chance to quiet down before I suddenly spoke out with a booming voice. The others just looked at me, stunned. Nobody in the room had ever heard me speak so forcefully like this before.

"Tommy, do you know how many years I have dragged along and carried the emotional baggage of what you inflicted on me as a kid? Well, for once and for all, we're going to go outside and settle the score. All of us are going to go outside right now and they're going to watch what I do to you to make up for what you did to me."

You should have seen Carl. He could have received an Academy Award for his stunning performance that evening. "Everybody, I know Bill well. He means business. Follow me outside!"

Everybody reluctantly got up and followed Carl outside, not knowing what to expect. Everyone, that is, except Tommy.

"NOW, TOMMY!" OUTSIDE!" I ordered in my sternest military voice.

Our ploy was working like a charm! Before any of the others could react, I firmly took Tommy by the arm and literally shoved him out of the back door into the alley behind the building. The others were completely confused. None of them had expected an evening quite like this.

Some of the others in the restaurant followed us outside and a crowd quickly gathered around the two of us, fully expecting a bloody scene.

Tommy didn't know what to do. He was expecting the very worst. He just timidly stood there, shaking, about to cry.

To the surprise of everyone, including Tommy, my whole demeanor suddenly changed. Before anybody could react, I briskly walked up and gave Tommy a hearty bear hug. "Tommy, I'd like to be your friend! A lot of water has flowed over our dams throughout the years. Each of us has better things to do than carry around any burdensome grudges from our school days. This life is too short for such nonsense. Come on, let's be friends."

Tommy's eyes grew larger as what I was saying to him began to sink in. For a fleeting moment, I thought he was going to collapse.

"Here," I said. "Why don't we sit next to each other at dinner so we can get caught up with each other? Carl and I want to tell you about some job ideas for you that Carl has pursued."

At the restaurant that night, there wasn't a dry eye in the place. Tommy and I visited and carried on as if we had been lifelong friends.

In the following days, Carl and I were able to finally get a job for Tommy at the local school. He became one of the school janitors, and from that day forward, he became an accepted and welcomed member of our town.

He even began sharing the same kindness with others that he had received that night at the restaurant. And the kindness he showed to the children at school more than made up for his bullying days at that same school those many years ago.

◆————————◆

*And be kind to one another, tenderhearted,*
*forgiving one another,*
*even as God in Christ forgave you.*
Ephesians 4:32

Forgiveness doesn't always come easy. It sure wasn't easy for me during all those years after being the victim of a bully. When you have been hurt by someone else, whether intentionally or unintentionally, saying "I forgive you," can become three of the most difficult words you've ever said.

Jesus knew what that was like. He was beaten, whipped, nailed to a cross, and hung up to die. And He was perfectly innocent. Yet, while He was hanging on the cross, He looked up to Father God and said, "Forgive them. They don't know what they are doing."

That has always been amazing to me. His love for his accusers allowed Him to overcome any concern whether they deserved His forgiveness or not. But it's not surprising, because He was just like His Heavenly Father.

God looks at us and He sees all of our failings, our sins, and our rebellion. He even knows that it was because of our sin that His Son Jesus had to die. He knows everything about us, and He still says, "I forgive you."

If you are a child of God, then you should be acting just like your Heavenly Father. Forgive those who have hurt you. They don't need to ask for your forgiveness first. (They might not even know they hurt you.) And you don't need to say it directly to them. But you do need to say it to God. When you do, He will remove that weight you've been carrying around for so long, and replace it with His peace.

*I shall pass through this world but once. Any good, therefore, that I can do or any kindness I can show to any human being, let me do it now. Let me not defer it or neglect it, for I shall not pass this way again.*

Stephen Grellet
Clergyman

# 8

# AN UNEXPECTED ENCOUNTER

*My idea surprised everyone . . . including me.*

One evening last fall I tearfully informed my treasured wife Bonnie that I was getting to the point where I would be forced to sell my home (we keep up two houses). My MS had deteriorated to the point where I could no longer keep up the house where I mainly office. Years ago, before I was diagnosed with multiple sclerosis, I had built this home myself, acting as my own general contractor. Wonderful memories from my years of living in it often preoccupy me.

The very next evening, as I was driving home with a friend of mine, we passed a church where I used to attend. As I got closer, we noticed a car parked out on the far edge of the parking lot. That in itself was not unusual, but we were surprised to see a shirtless guy walking toward his car.

"Tyler," I said to my friend. "Let's drive over there and see what's happening. I wonder what he's up to."

"I don't know, Billy," Ty replied. "I don't feel comfortable with that. What if it's a drug drop-off? They might have guns."

But I had a strong sense that we were supposed to continue and I wasn't going to be swayed. We slowly drove up and motioned for this young man to come over to our car. We introduced ourselves and asked if he needed any help. I was immediately put at ease by his friendly manner and it soon became obvious that he had nothing to hide. A young woman, his wife, got out of their car and came over to greet us.

Our intention was simply to find out why they were parked there, but our conversation quickly became much more personal as they shared their story with us.

Their names were Justin and Elizabeth, and they told us they were former drug addicts and had recently left Oregon in order to get away from the unsavory people and lifestyle that had trapped them. They had almost gotten divorced, and that brought them to the realization that they would both be in danger if they continued to stay there.

They were trying to decide if they should head to Louisiana or Minnesota when a friend of theirs told them he could get them jobs and a temporary place to live in Minneapolis. So they stashed what little belongings they had in their car and started their 1900-mile journey. They weren't sure if their car would even make it, but Justin had been a mechanic and they stopped every 300 miles so he could check things out and keep the car going.

Elizabeth told us that while they were on the road, they had been having the best talks of their 12 years together. They had become much closer and their marriage was stronger than it had ever been, in spite of their circumstances. They both attributed this to asking Jesus to guide them.

As their car had limped from one town to another, and with a refuse-to-lose attitude, they shouted out to God. To them, their shouts had become the "Team Green Rally Cry."

Unfortunately, when they were less than 200 miles from Minneapolis, their friend who had promised them the world, called and timidly admitted that he had no jobs lined up for them. To make matters worse, his wife had put her foot down and said she didn't want Justin and Elizabeth to stay with them.

"The very next morning," explained Justin, "we stopped by this church and introduced ourselves. The kind pastor and his congregation helped by getting us a workable car and let us temporarily park over here. We're pretty enterprising people, and we both got jobs right away, but we haven't had a place to stay so we've been sleeping here in our car for more than two months.

"Just tonight I told Liz that we were spending our last night in Minneapolis. We'll probably head to Louisiana. We are both dead-set against moving back to Oregon. Team Green has accepted we lost the game of life back there. We desperately need to start a new game and we just can't put up with the hassle of living in our car with the hot weather, mosquitoes, and storms."

*Hot weather. Mosquitoes. Storms.* As I heard those words I suddenly began to experience a vivid, horrid flashback to my time in Vietnam. Back in those terrifying days of combat, I had no place to peacefully rest my head at night. The best we soldiers could do was muster enough energy in the sweltering heat to dig our "two-by-two-by-you" foxholes. Unfortunately, they would be filled up with water in five minutes during the monsoon season, and we only had our poncho liners to protect our faces from the hordes of mosquitoes.

In that ungodly setting, I dreamed of making it home alive so I could have a safe place to live without having to move each night. I wanted a home that could be a haven for people in need. All I wanted was a dog to rest its head on my lap as I relaxed in a rocking chair on my front porch.

As I came back to the reality of the moment, I suddenly realized that Justin and Elizabeth were in much the same predicament that I had been in, and I knew exactly how they were feeling.

Now, an unlikely idea was overwhelming me. As I thought about it for a moment, I realized it was the Holy Spirit leading me.

Tyler was stunned as he heard me say, "Hey you two. Would you like to shower up and be able to sleep in a comfy bed, at least for tonight? Follow me over to my house."

As I was driving home with them following me, I started to feel a little uneasy and began to think, *Shiebs, what have you done?* But I quickly rejected that thinking and knew that God's timing was perfect. Just 12 hours before they were going to leave Minneapolis, God had arranged this meeting and I took them in.

Just the other day Justin and I were reminiscing about that first meeting. He said to me, "You think you were sizing us up? You had no idea how skeptical Elizabeth and I were of you. Bill, you came out of nowhere and offered to help us. Why would you have done that? What benefit did you hope to get? To this day, we still shake our heads at your unabashed kindness."

At first, I offered to have them stay overnight, but our friendship quickly grew and one night became two and then became a week. During that time, Bonnie and I found ourselves holding hands with Justin and Liz as we said grace together over one of our new-found candlelight dinners.

The time seemed to fly by so fast, and I was having so much fun having them in my home that I asked them to stay with me over the winter. One day shortly after that, I came home to find a beautiful, framed print sitting atop one of my stereo speakers. It read, *"Angels exist, but sometimes they don't have wings and are called friends."*

As I stood there, eyes glistening, Justin and Liz simultaneously hugged me, remarking, "Thank you for helping start our lives anew! We couldn't have done this if it wasn't for you and the Holy Spirit acting on our behalf."

Not long after that, Elizabeth asked me if I would be offended if they got a dog. To this day I don't think she had any idea how cheerful my reaction would be. I had always wanted a dog, but had slowly grown to accept that I couldn't care for one because of my MS.

They began their search and found an animal shelter with a dog that was within one day of being put down. Before we knew it, Diesel, all 120 pounds of him, was making himself at home as we fed him scraps from the dinner table. He is a gentle giant (half Labrador and half mastiff), and all the kids in our neighborhood have become his friend. He has become my steadfast companion and whenever I am resting, he licks my ear and snuggles beside me.

Bonnie asked Justin and Elizabeth to join our family for Christmas this past winter. Our extended family of 23 people had a wonderful time together. Liz admitted that it was Bonnie's kindness of warmly welcoming them into the family that finally convinced the two of them that they are indeed enjoying a gift from God.

Shortly after our holiday gathering, Bonnie broke down and cried with joy when I asked her if I could let Justin and Liz live here indefinitely. Not only had she become close to them, but she was so relieved. Our entire family had been talking about who could care for Grandpa Bill because it had reached the point where I couldn't care for myself.

My act of kindness was soon passed on to others as well. This past spring, Justin and Liz took their first vacation and drove down to Nashville, Tennessee. While there, they were deeply touched when they came upon a homeless camp.

The place was in absolute squalor. There were no shelters, no tents, and little children were running around with no one watching them. The sight overwhelmed Justin and Liz, and they both broke down in tears.

Justin turned to Liz and said, "Honey, this could have been us. We have to do something."

After a quick prayer, Justin crossed the street and stepped into the midst of the camp while Liz stayed back. Almost at once, he was surrounded by a dozen people who made it clear they didn't want him around.

But Justin has guts. He smiled at them and said, "Two years ago my wife and I were homeless, living in our car, when a man came out of nowhere and offered us a helping hand. I'm here today to offer some help to you. We're staying at a motel down the road. If any of you would like to come over, take a shower, and get out of this miserable heat for awhile, we'd like to offer our place to you. After we finish supper, we'll come back with a few sandwiches for you. I know this won't solve all your problems, but it's the best we can do."

By the looks on their faces, he could tell they didn't really believe him. Soon, though, one young couple came forward to accept their offer, and the four of them ended up having some deep conversations.

When Justin and Liz came back home and told me their story, Justin piped up and said, "Bill, even though only two came forward out of the bunch, we believe we sowed some seeds of hope, especially when we brought back those sandwiches. We've even become Facebook friends with that couple, and we think they sincerely want to change their life.

"Look at what you did for us. It's like throwing a stone into some water. It might just be a little stone, but the ripples keep going out and out. You took a chance with helping us. We took a chance with helping others.

"We passed on your kindness, and with God's help it worked, Bill. It worked!"

After almost three years together, Justin and Elizabeth have moved on to a warmer climate and stepped into the next chapter of their life together. My simple gesture of kindness has paid off for ALL of us, simply because we were willing to listen to God and turn our cares and concerns over to Him.

◆——————————◆

*"I was hungry and you gave Me food;*
*I was thirsty and you gave Me drink;*
*I was a stranger and you took Me in;*
*I was naked and you clothed Me;*
*I was sick and you visited Me;*
*I was in prison and you came to Me."*
Matthew 25:35-36

When it comes to examining your life, I find this to be one of the most challenging passages in the Bible. It describes the time of the return of Jesus, when He gathers all the people together and explains the good that some of them had done. In fact, He is describing what they had done for Him.

The people began to look back at their lives and question Him, saying they had never seen Him in any of those situations, and they wondered when they had done those things. Then Jesus responds with an almost shocking statement.

"When you did these things for the lowliest people you encountered, you did them to Me."

Jesus is reminding us that all people – without exception – have been made in the image of God. And we are called to demonstrate the goodness of God and show kindness to people whenever it is in our power to do so. In other words, we are to do for them what Jesus would do if He was standing with them.

I don't know about you, but that's not necessarily an easy thing for me to always do. When I meet someone that I know nothing about, or someone whose appearance makes me question if I should turn around and run, the easiest thing is to simply smile and continue on with my day. But I can't.

There was a book written more than 100 years ago called, *In His Steps*, by Charles Sheldon. It's the story of a group of people who commit to live their lives by asking one simple question whenever they had a decision to make. That question is the same one my mother taught me so many years ago: What would Jesus do?

Asking that question, then following the Holy Spirit's guidance, has led me on adventure after adventure throughout my life. I would challenge and encourage you to do the same. Jesus is waiting to reach out with you. All you have to do is follow in His steps.

# CONCLUSION

## *You can do it too!*

You may look at some of the things I've done and think, *I could never do that.* And you would be right, because you're not me. But I couldn't do some of the things you do either.

The truth is, God has given each person unique gifts, strengths, and personalities. He uses those, along with our experiences, to enable us to do things that most other people couldn't – or wouldn't. Let me tell you a little more about what makes me tick.

Multiple sclerosis. Even though I've been saddled with it for years, the very mention of those two words still strikes uneasiness in my heart. A lingering question I ask myself is, "How bad am I going to get?"

Although I try to be cheerful as I interact with others, deep down inside I wrestle every day with a fear that seems to always be nagging at me, eating away at my innards. Most people, while they observe my cheerfulness, fail to realize the feeling of apprehension that dwells within my once-healthy body. Some extend kind words to me. "Bill, just think; when you reach heaven, you'll get a brand new healthy body. You'll be able to run and play sports with the rest of us!"

Inside I think, *Well, that's wonderful, but in the meantime, what am I going to do today?*

Years ago on one frigid morning in the middle of winter in Minnesota, I struggled to get out of bed. A bitterly cold morning with sub-zero temperatures blasted me in the face as I attempted to step outside. The roads were icy, and I wondered how I was going to drive out to the VA hospital. I was concerned that I was about to go careening all over the highway.

Though my drive was dicey, by God's grace I made my way to the hospital without having an accident. After I struggled to walk across the icy parking lot, I continued a halting journey to my appointment, aided by my two walking canes.

As I waited for the doctor to come into my room, I peered out of the window and noticed a delivery truck driver briskly walking into the hospital. For a few moments I envied his physical ability as he nonchalantly carried a large parcel into the building.

Suddenly I felt a gentle hand resting on my shoulder, and I looked up. Here was my favorite neurologist, Dr. Alex, grinning from ear-to-ear.

"Mr. Schiebler," he began. "I've been quietly standing behind you for a few moments, looking at that same delivery man. I've had some trying days myself when I look out at him as he delivers his packages, thinking that I'd like to trade places with that young man.

"So, what's happening to you this morning? I notice that you only have on one sock. Are you getting so hard up that, as you've joked before, you've had to mortgage your pet cobra

Fang?"

That morning, only he could get me laughing.

"Dr. Alex, I'm just having one of those mornings. I attempted to put on my right sock for 21 minutes, but to no avail. It was so frustrating that I actually timed it. Though some days are diamonds and others are stones, my day so far has been a rock."

To my astonishment, he started grinning even more when he heard my forlorn bellyaching.

"Well, Mr. Schiebler, look at your plight this way. There are plenty of other people who are worse off than you. You're fortunate that you've not only been able to get out of your bed, you were able to walk to your car. Furthermore, in spite of the this bad weather, somehow you've managed to drive all the way out here this morning. If you followed me on my rounds today, you'd encounter many people who are worse off than you.

"It's all in the way that you look at your life."

Dr. Alex, wherever you are these days, thanks for showing me how to have a better attitude. The lesson about acceptance you taught me that day literally turned my life around and steered me in a much more productive direction.

His advice encouraged me and, I believe, reinforced my ability to use unconventional ways of coping with life. I decided I didn't want to merely exist. I was determined to thrive.

Come what may, the traits of *creativity, tenacity,* and *eccentricity* were to become hallmarks in my life and help make my life much more enjoyable.

Along the way, I have learned some hard lessons from a number of trials I have faced. Fortunately, I have been able to use those lessons to help mold my thinking to come up with different ideas and creative ways to make my life better. They've helped me make other people's lives better, as well.

CREATIVITY

As I look back on my life, I realize that I was already fashioning things and coming up with some unorthodox ideas as a youngster.

It seems like only yesterday when I overheard my mother (who taught gifted children in Boston) visiting with her friend, Mavis. The two were chatting in our driveway. I was around the corner of the house in our backyard building a toy out of a spare wooden orange crate. Out of curiosity, I snuck up to eavesdrop on what she was telling her friend. I heard a proud mother sharing about her wayward son (me), the one who turned out a bit different from her other two children.

"Mavis, you and I are close enough friends so I can share some things about our middle son Bill. Of our three children, he is the most content with playing by himself. Carl (my dad) and I have figured out that Bill has to compensate because of his frail health. He can't play team sports like baseball or football like the other children, because he just doesn't have the coordination or strength to compete.

"He's content to play alone out in the fields by the railroad tracks. In fact, he just built an underground fort over there that is the envy of his friends. Bill figured out a way to use a large pine tree stump to hide the entrance. When they move that stump, he and his friends climb down into a tunnel that leads to the main room.

"When we first heard about this, we were concerned," my mother continued. "We thought he had tunneled under the ground and the dirt roof could collapse on him. So one night when Bill came home for supper, Carl discreetly walked over to take a close look at his fort.

"It turned out Bill hadn't dug a dirt tunnel. He had hauled eight-foot wooden logs from the paper mill log piles to make the roof for his fort. Then, he laid piled clumps of grass over the logs so no one would know his fort is there. Carl has never seen the likes of it."

It felt wonderful to listen to my proud mother talk about me, and I think it cemented in me the importance of being creative. Over the years, that trait has come to the forefront in my life time and again whenever I was faced with an unfamiliar situation or the desire to somehow be kind to the person in front of me.

## TENACITY

When I was a kid, all of my friends used to play marbles, and every kid had his own special bag of them. My bag was filled with over 50 marbles I had collected.

One time, my buddy Art's dad brought home a big steely (a one-inch ball bearing) from the large paper mill in town. (What does a marble player do with a steely? Anything he wants to.) When he gave it to Art, I knew I was going to be in a run for my money.

Before I knew it, Art had used his newly acquired steely to wipe me out. And he did it in just one game. Out of the kindness of his heart, he had left me with two marbles. I dragged myself home with my tail between my legs, sulking all the way.

When I got home, I took my now-much-lighter bag of marbles and flipped it dejectedly underneath my bed. For two days all I did was mope around the house. But then I had an idea. I asked Art's dad to bring home another ball bearing so I could have one too. Now I was back in the game and wiping out my other buddies. Before long, I had regained even more marbles than I had before.

In my family-dispute mediation work, I've noticed that some people just give up on life. When they get wiped out in their "marble game," they lament and slink home. Then they crawl into a corner after throwing their practically-empty bag of marbles underneath their bed – out of sight – never to muster up the courage to play another game of "marbles" again.

My marble experience taught me a valuable lesson in tenacity – of never giving up. Throughout my life I have made a very purposeful, conscious decision to never quit trying, no matter what obstacles I faced.

The lesson I learned from toughing it out as I played those marble games as a youngster surfaced again when I went through the Army's rigorous Ranger training. Each morning those sadistic, paratrooper-jumpmasters burst into our rooms and hollered for us to line up within three minutes to begin our daily excruciating, ten-mile all-out run (not a jog).

During those runs, they'd holler out, "If I can do it, you can do it!" Every Ranger-to-be would chant back, "If you can do, I can do it!"

One day at the end of our run, to our utter surprise, instead of stopping us at the black and yellow striped poles that indicated the end, those jumpmasters ran us a short 100 yards beyond where we expected our run to end.

In that short final burst of energy, more would-be Rangers fell out of formation (and lost the chance to be a Ranger) than we had lost during the entire ten-mile run. It became apparent that they had not set their sights high enough, and when faced with putting in that extra effort, they couldn't do it.

Very few Army volunteers for Ranger training completed the nine week, utterly exhausting Ranger course. I was never pushed to my physical limits as much in combat as I was during Ranger training. On one long-range patrol, we trudged non-stop through parts of three states while being forced to stay awake for five days and nights.

Enduring combat became the ultimate test of tenacity. I could write a book about how we were forced to tough it out. No tents, no buildings, just our foxholes. Any way of living after combat was a lifestyle for which we were grateful.

Then came my diagnosis of MS. Neurologists curtly stated, "You have the type of multiple sclerosis where you will most likely be confined to a wheelchair by the time you are 50 years old. Surely by the time you reach age 55."

But I was able to walk with canes until I became 76 years old. For that 21-year freebie, I want to say, "Thank You, Jesus."

## ECCENTRICITY

Wheelchair-bound people face many of the same problems, regardless of their disease. When they become confined to a wheelchair, most people never venture out to walk again. Instead, they just give up.

Obviously, my case of MS differs from others and I can only speak for myself, but perhaps I can share a few lessons I've learned about following some eccentric ideas. The concept of either using a wheelchair or walking is a hurdle I have overcome. I thought, *Why can't I use a wheelchair* and *walk?* When I am home, I have devised a means with unorthodox creativity whereby I don't have to use my wheelchair. I walk throughout my house.

My friends remarked, "Bill, you've had some crazy and eccentric ideas before, but your latest scheme really takes the cake."

Back when I was a Ranger, I kept a six-foot length of nylon cliff rappelling rope that I had used when I taught mountaineering. Little did I realize that 50 years later this very Swiss seat belt, as they were called, would dangle from the ceiling less than a foot away from my desk up here in my north office.

Throughout my house, I have hung 89 of these cliff rappelling ropes from carabiners attached to my ceiling joists (one for each jump I made as a paratrooper). Each rope has a couple sturdy knots tied in them so I can grab the rope to give myself the balance and support I need as I walk throughout my house. Rope-by-rope and step-by-step. I am free to walk around my house wherever I want to go.

At first, my occupational and physical therapists at the VA scoffed at my idea. Then they heard how astonished my radiologist friend Dr. Mike became after he saw all my ropes dangling in the house. He remarked, "Bill, my mother is suffering from Parkinson's disease and hasn't walked for several years. I can't believe what I'm seeing here. You can walk anywhere in your house without assistance. Would you mind if I take some pictures of this?"

"Of course," I replied. "I would be honored if you did."

After he left my house, he stopped at a couple stores on the way home and picked up the material he would need to do this very same thing in his mother's house.

The result? Mike's mother cried off and on for three days because those ropes enabled her to walk for the first time in over seven years.

Those cliff rappelling ropes may seem a bit eccentric to you, but they have been the most helpful adaptation I have ever devised.

Why do I tell you all this about me? Because like me, God has given you something special that you can use to show kindness to anyone you come in contact with. How you do it will be unique for every person and every situation, and it will probably stretch you a bit (or a lot) as you simply show that you're willing to do what you can to make someone's life better. But God is infinitely creative and is ready to guide you every step of the way.

That's been my experience as I've listened and looked for some way to show kindness to the people I meet.

As you finish reading this book, perhaps you're thinking, *I wonder what the kindest thing would be that Bill could do for me?*

Let me answer your question with one last story.

For years I had been quite rebellious. While I had always believed in God, my spiritual wrestling match revolved around who this Jesus Christ was.

Fortunately, many people kept coming into my life who would demonstrate God's love and kindness, not just toward the world in general, but specifically toward me.

They hung in there with me in good times and bad until I finally came to accept that Jesus had died for my sins. By His death, He had made a way, the only way, for me to receive forgiveness from my own sins, and accept His gift of salvation.

There is no time for lingering guilt if one is truly a Christian. Christ died for you, and if you repent of your sins, your Heavenly Father will not only forgive you, but He will then purposefully forget every sin you committed. Your guilt will be washed away.

You might not agree with my views, but that's all right. Fortunately, we live in a great country where many have fought and died just so we could have the freedom to agree or disagree. Each of us has the right to our own personal views. But no matter where you are in the journey of your life, whether you are rebellious (as I was) or simply unsure, God loves you.

My wish is that you can accept all that Jesus Christ did for you, so He can become your Savior, your Lord, and your closest Friend. *That's the greatest kindness I can do for you.*

◆————————————◆

*For God so loved the world*
*that He gave His only begotten Son,*
*that whoever believes in Him should not perish*
*but have everlasting life.*
John 3:16

# AFTERWORD

## Heartfelt Memories of My Meeting With the Eisenhowers.

My late father was too young to fight in World War I but too old to fight in World War II. Instead, he represented the paper industry during the Second World War. My Dad emerged from serving on the War Production Board with wariness. He became very apprehensive about our nation's developing pre-occupation with the so-called *military industrial complex*.

The morning I was about to depart for Vietnam, Dad broke down. He was especially upset about my involvement in this new war in Vietnam.

The very spot at the end of our driveway where we both stood to say our goodbyes to each other remains etched in my mind. With tears in his eyes, he managed to utter some disturbing words: "Why are you doing this to your mother and me?"

His provocative question caught me off guard. I was unable to answer him.

In Vietnam, I was wounded the first time when one of our men opened fire on my patrol as we returned to friendly lines late at night after engaging the enemy.

There I was, a restless patient staring up at the ceiling, bedridden in a mobile Army surgical hospital (MASH) tent.

Suddenly, an idea overwhelmed me. I struggled to get up, hobbled over to the nurse's table and softly asked the medics in our hospital tent,

"Do you guys have a typewriter I can work with for a couple of hours?"

A medic responded, "Sure. There's one right over there. We use it for day reports. Nobody uses it at night. You can use it, but just be finished by dawn."

That question my father asked had stuck with me, and my thoughts had jelled about "why" I was fighting in Vietnam. I sat down and wrote an idealistic letter back to my dad. (Since then, I have made a 180 degree turnaround about my views toward the Vietnam War.)

As fathers proudly do, he showed my letter to his cronies at the paper mill. Somebody made a copy and forwarded it to the local small town newspaper.

Wouldn't you know it, almost at once, the AP (Associated Press) and UPI (United Press International) picked up my story and reprinted it in newspapers throughout the country.

Little did I know how the distribution of that letter would impact me while I was still in Vietnam.

Returning to base camp after being subjected to excruciating firefights was a somber affair. Our men just sat there with blank looks on their faces. Each peered at nearby empty bunks, obviously wondering if theirs would soon be empty.

Something had to immediately be done to cheer up my men, so my first task was to go down to the company mail tent with my radio telephone operator to get our platoon's mail. Hopefully, a letter from home would cheer them up.

As we departed the mail tent, a mail clerk stopped me. "Sir, aren't you going to get your mail?"

"Well, yeah, I've already got our platoon mail," I replied.

"Nope, Sir. Shouldn't you take your own mail, too?" he asked.

Dumbfounded, I retorted, "I've already got my platoon's mail."

"Sir, you need to take your personal mail, too."

For the life of me, I didn't realize what was happening. We dragged back two duffle bags full of mail. After examining my own mail, I found more than 350 encouraging letters from all over the country from people who had read the article I had written to my dad.

Two letters really stuck out from the group. One was from Waldheim Circle in Pittsburgh, from General Matthew Ridgway. In case you didn't know, after President Harry Truman fired General Douglas MacArthur in Korea, General Ridgway was appointed MacArthur's successor. (Upon returning to the U.S., I was able to spend the afternoon with him and his wife at their home.)

The other letter, though, completely mystified me. I looked on the back of the envelope and it said, "General and Mrs. Dwight D. Eisenhower." (After he retired from the presidency, Eisenhower preferred to be called "General.") Inside was a one page letter telling me how much he and his wife had enjoyed my article and wishing me a safe return from combat.

Without sharing it with anyone else, I discreetly stashed it away in the bottom of my footlocker.

Unfortunately, my eyes never got the chance to examine that letter again. Two weeks later when we returned from yet another operation, our platoon found a crater where our troop tent had been. An enemy mortar round had scored a direct hit on our tent, obliterating it and everything in it.

Oh well.

Thoughts about losing their kind letter still bothered me, though. When I returned from Vietnam and arrived in Los Angeles, I arranged to have a military telephone operator call the Eisenhower compound in Gettysburg, Pennsylvania. Unfortunately, the operator in Gettysburg said the General had suffered several heart attacks and was recuperating at his winter residency in Palm Springs, California. She then transferred my call to his winter home.

When a secretary answered the phone, I asked whether I could meet with the General to at least say hello and thank him for his kind letter.

She tersely informed me that such a meeting wouldn't be possible. Eisenhower was booked out over eight weeks in advance. But unexpectedly, she put me on hold to confer with his appointment secretary.

It seemed like hours before she returned to the phone. I anxiously stood there thinking, *Lady, come on, get going! I've only got so many dimes and quarters.*

When she returned to the phone, though, her demeanor had changed. "Well, here's a departure from his normal schedule. The General has a cancellation. He could fit you in for a few minutes." At that news, I almost fell over in shock!

"When's the cancellation?" I quickly asked.

"Today," she calmly replied.

My hopes were dashed. "Well, I can't get down there upon such short notice. I'm way up here in Los Angeles!"

"Now, don't you worry," she continued. "We've got hourly commuter flights out of L.A. to Palm Springs. If you can make flight arrangements, we'll send somebody to the airport to pick you up."

When I hung up the phone and phoned my dad, he immediately wired the money for the ticket to the airline's desk. Years later, neighbors of my folks asked about why the Secret Service was checking me out. Apparently, they had immediately responded to check my background, even though I already had a secret-level clearance from being in the Army.

My life that day flashed by as if in a whirlwind. When my plane landed at the airport, what seemed to me like a huge, half-mile long limousine with 35 doors on each side, drove right up to the plane's boarding ramp.

Before anybody deplaned, the limousine driver walked up the stairs, got on the microphone, and said, "Is there a Lieutenant

Schiebler onboard?"

Slumping down in my seat, I raised my hand. "Right here," I sheepishly answered.

As I walked down the plane's aisle, people looked at me in wonderment. When we got off the plane I asked the driver, "Sir, I've never ridden in a limousine before. Is it all right with you if I sit up front?"

"Sure, this will be great," he responded. "Then I can turn on the radio."

As we left the airport to head out to the Eisenhower compound, people gawked as we drove by. There weren't very many limousines back in those days.

When we arrived at the compound, a medical doctor and a couple of nurses greeted me with cautionary looks on their faces. "Now, the General has suffered a series of heart attacks. We don't want you to mention any subject that might agitate him. You are not to even mention the word *Vietnam*. The General gets worked up when he hears that word."

Not to be outdone, I blurted out, "Oh no, not me. I wouldn't even mention such a word!"

They ushered me into a small drawing room, and I stood there, uneasily fidgeting with straightening my tie. Those next few moments seemed like ages to me.

Suddenly, in walked President Eisenhower. He warmly greeted me, and I stood at attention. "Mr. President, sir, I don't even know how to address you."

Flashing that well-known million-dollar smile of his, he said, "Well, we're both military men. I prefer 'General.' At ease, Lieutenant Schiebler." (He even pronounced my last name properly.)

"Sir," I began, "you and my father have something in common. You both are golfers." (His compound was right on the edge of a golf course.)

He retorted, "They haven't let me play golf since my heart attacks. Come in here and I'll show you an enjoyable hobby I've been dabbling with."

We walked into an adjoining room that held a number of art easels. He cheerfully commented, "I really enjoy art. Look, here's a painting of a barn I just finished. Last week, I got some limited prints of it and I'll have one of my staff members give you one."

Folks, I may be dumb but I'm not stupid. This time, no mortar round was going to obliterate this painting I received from him. Right now, I'm upstairs here in a small office above my garage and looking at his painting of a barn. In my view, Eisenhower was a good novice artist. For you artists, he did a superb job with putting things into three-point perspective.

Now, to put the icing on the cake, in walked his wife Mamie. What a delightful, down-to-earth lady. "Mrs. Eisenhower, you and my mother have something in common," I said. "Flowers."

She beamed, "You two follow me out here. I want to show you my flower gardens. See those milkweed pods? They attract monarch butterflies."

Blushing, I admitted, "Mrs. Eisenhower, I'm afraid I don't know much about flowers. In fact, I can't tell the difference between petunias and pansies."

She laughed and remarked with a giggle, "Oh you two. Neither of you boys know much about gardening."

When she blurted out the word *boy*, I was dumbfounded. This seemed like an amazing statement to me. I thought to myself, *Lady, you have to be the only person in this world who could call a two-term president and one of only eight five-star generals in the United States, a boy!*

Mind you, my visit with the Eisenhowers was supposed to last only 15 minutes. The three of us walked back in and sat down in the drawing room. He popped right up, "I'll bet they wouldn't permit you to talk about that war over there, would they?"

With due respect, I forcefully replied, "Oh no, sir, they wouldn't even permit me to say the word."

President Eisenhower became unglued. "Well, I'm going to talk about it. We're going to lose this one. They could put machine guns on every street corner over there, but we're still going to lose this one. You might recall how often I've talked about not getting embroiled within the military industrial complex. We need to fight the battles and get out instead of wasting our time and effort building a complex that looks like we're moving in. Our ratio of fighting men to back-up logistical support is 1-to-10. Theirs is 10-to-1. Nope, we're going to lose this one.

"Mamie and I invited you to come and visit us because we

both were deeply impressed with the article you wrote to your father explaining your patriotism to him and why you felt justified with fighting in Vietnam. Unfortunately, we are fighting guerilla warfare with outdated World War II tactics over there.

"In Vietnam, there are no battle lines. In World War II, at least there were battle lines with good people on one side, bad people on the other side. The war in Vietnam has become one for assessing body counts. Winning the war against the teeming masses in the Orient has nothing to do with body counts."

His face softened as he looked at me. "Getting back to why we invited you to visit us. It's quite obvious that you write with your heart. We hope you will develop your writing skills. Thank you for coming down here from Los Angeles to visit us."

It was my turn to speak up. "Sir and Mrs. Eisenhower, I'm just a young 24-year-old, but I want to thank you both for giving me the thrill of my lifetime. May God richly bless and watch over you and your family."

They both grinned and the General responded. "God bless you, too. We so hope you will be able to readjust from the horrors you have been through. Both of us hope you will lead a productive life."

Staff members gave me a print of his painting and ushered me out of the compound. As I reached the limousine the driver remarked, "I'll bet you want to ride back to the airport in the front seat again."

When we arrived and he stopped to let me depart, onlookers

gazed with curiosity as I walked back into the airport. I just raised my arm and greeted them, "Hello folks. The driver and I are just friends." They looked away and went on with their business.

As for me, I walked back into the airport and went on with my life, never forgetting the kindness shown to me by General Dwight Eisenhower and his wife Mamie.

# ABOUT THE AUTHOR

Bill Schiebler has a ferocious tenacity that reminds people of that rabbit in the Energizer commercials: he just keeps banging away. Those who know Bill, kid him as being not a survivalist, but an overcomer.

As a child, he suffered from whooping cough and respiratory illnesses that left him unable to join his friends in team sports, so he played alone out in the fields of his hometown in Wisconsin.

When he was old enough, he began biking from one yard job to another with a small wheelbarrow balanced on his handlebars. Somehow, Bill often had eleven yard jobs at once in the small town where he grew up.

By the time he was in high school, he was competing in swimming and track.

Back in 1965, American involvement in the war over in Vietnam was expanding. Bill had already become a paratrooper in the Army Rangers. He fought in some of the most horrific battles of the war and was wounded multiple times. Schiebler was awarded the Bronze Star for Valor when he carried a North Vietnamese prisoner on his back for over three miles in enemy territory as he struggled to re-enter friendly lines.

Schiebler challenged himself at every turn, and doors of opportunity opened to him. He successfully climbed to the summit of the Matterhorn in Switzerland, had a unique meeting with President Dwight Eisenhower and his wife Mamie, and through the years developed lasting friendships with such people as Norman Vincent Peale's wife Ruth Stafford Peale, Zig Ziglar, and General Norman Schwarzkopf, to name just a few.

He began noticing some perplexing medical symptoms, though. To his utter dismay, neurologists informed him that he had displayed classic symptoms of multiple sclerosis since eighth grade. He wasn't diagnosed with the illness until 19 years later after being discharged from active duty in the army.

Upon receiving his belated diagnosis, Bill was mystified! He had gone through very physically challenging experiences throughout his life while being afflicted with early symptoms of MS.

In spite of his physically demanding drawbacks, today he still stays actively involved in the lives of people as a family dispute mediator, helping them to overcome their difficulties just as he has overcome his.

He is married, with seven children, 13 grandchildren, two great-grandchildren, and lives in Minnesota.

# A FINAL NOTE

Bill Schiebler sums up his life this way:

*If they came along today, shackled my hands with handcuffs and ushered me out of this big hallway of life's excitement, I'd say it has all been well worth it.*

*Jesus, thank You so much for creating me!*

To get more of Bill's books or to follow his blog, go to:

# www.billschiebler.com